W9-CLH-942

"These are essential and liberating tools to transform habits—practical, simple, and wise."

—**Jack Kornfield**, author of *A Path with Heart*

"If you can bring your habitual patterns of thinking and acting into an accepting, kind, and mindful presence, you have the key to happiness and peace. Hugh Byrne's brilliant new book on habits guides you in this pathway, applying mindfulness to some of our most difficult, persistent, and unhealthy habits. Please read and share with others…these teachings are a gift to all who seek inner freedom."

—**Tara Brach**, author of *Radical Acceptance* and *Radical Compassion*

"The foundation of *Habit Swap* is that an untrained mind is the root cause of our suffering, and that the untrained mind almost always functions on autopilot or in a state of unawareness. Through his thorough exploration of mindfulness practices, Byrne shows how to lift the veil of unawareness to make what was invisible visible, leading to happiness and a sense of who we really are."

—**Sharon Salzberg**, author of *Lovingkindness* and *Real Happiness*

HABIT SWAP

TRADE in YOUR UNHEALTHY HABITS for MINDFUL ONES

HUGH G. BYRNE, PHD

New Harbinger Publications, Inc.

Publisher's Note

Distributed in Canada by Raincoast Books

Copyright © 2020 by Hugh G. Byrne
New Harbinger Publications, Inc.
5674 Shattuck Avenue
Oakland, CA 94609
www.newharbinger.com

Cover design by Amy Shoup; Acquired by Jess O'Brien;
Edited by Marisa Solis

Library of Congress Cataloging-in-Publication Data

Names: Byrne, Hugh G., author.
Title: Habit swap : trade in your unhealthy habits for mindful ones / Hugh G. Byrne.
Description: Oakland, CA : New Harbinger Publications, [2020] | Includes bibliographical references.
Identifiers: LCCN 2019055181 (print) | LCCN 2019055182 (ebook) | ISBN 9781684034086 (paperback) | ISBN 9781684034093 (pdf) | ISBN 9781684034109 (epub)
Subjects: LCSH: Habit breaking. | Self-control. | Mindfulness (Psychology)
Classification: LCC BF337.B74 B97 2020 (print) | LCC BF337.B74 (ebook) | DDC 158.1--dc23
LC record available at https://lccn.loc.gov/2019055181
LC ebook record available at https://lccn.loc.gov/2019055182

Printed in the United States of America

22   21   20

10   9   8   7   6   5   4   3   2   1   First Printing

To my late parents,
John and Kathleen Byrne,
with love and gratitude.

Contents

Introduction

The simple message of this book is that you can transform your life by changing your habits. And *mindfulness*—conscious awareness of your experience—is a key to changing your habits.

Mindfulness brings into conscious awareness habitual behaviors that have become automatic and unconscious through repetition—it makes what was invisible visible. We are then in a position to think, speak, and act in ways that lead to greater well-being and freedom. This is the promise of mindfulness when applied to letting go of unhealthy and unwanted habits and cultivating more beneficial ones.

In my previous book on mindfulness and habit change, *The Here-and-Now Habit* (Byrne 2016), I explored the science of habit formation and habit change—and why and how the cultivation and practice of mindfulness are a critical path to changing habits and living with greater freedom and ease.

In this book, we dig more deeply into ways of working mindfully with particular habits, from spending large swaths of time online to eating or drinking unconsciously to putting off important tasks, for example. We explore how we can let go of unhelpful habits and develop more beneficial ones. We look at how to bring mindfulness to both the *roots* of our habits and their *expressions* (behaviors). These skills help us identify and work with even the most entrenched habits.

Beyond skills, practices, and techniques—which are important and necessary—what mindfulness brings to our lives and to our effort to change habits is a way of being that creates the soil within which needed change can happen.

The spirit of mindfulness and the spirit with which we approach mindful habit change is one of *acceptance, compassion*, and *nonjudgment*:

- When we meet our habits with **acceptance**, we acknowledge the truth of our experience—even when it may be painful to accept. This becomes the place from which wise and necessary change can begin.

- Meeting our experience with **compassion**, we open space to our difficulties and the conditions that may have .contributed to them with kindness.

- With **nonjudgment**, we acknowledge things as they are and bring interest and curiosity to

what we're experiencing. With this greater
awareness, we're able to determine wise means
of responding.

In this spirit, there is not a "good" you trying to disci-
pline or change a "bad" you, or a stern taskmaster telling you
how you "should" be acting. Rather, with nonjudgmental
awareness, we can bring a compassionate understanding to
the ways in which all of us, given particular conditions and
experiences, can make choices that lead to harm. We can
see that our brains, programmed by thousands of years of
evolution, can at times abet us in forming habits that don't
ultimately benefit us. With this knowledge, we take responsibility for our actions and words without blame or harsh
judgment. We learn to take action that leads to our own and
others' well-being.

In the first three chapters, we present the promise of
mindfulness—and the power of meditation—in helping us
let go of unhealthy and unwanted habits and in developing
more beneficial ones.

In chapters 4 through 7, we engage with the roots of our
habits—wanting, aversion, distraction, and busyness—and
explore positive habits—acceptance, gratitude, compassion,
joy, and others—that help us move toward greater well-
being. We also focus on stress as we work with both the roots
and expressions of our habits.

In the remaining chapters, we work with the habitual behaviors as they are expressed, for example, in unhealthy eating, drinking, and consuming; unwise involvement with our devices and technology; our speech and communication; and procrastination and other unhelpful habits. We also explore ways of cultivating healthy antidotes to these behaviors.

I've practiced mindfulness for more than thirty years. One of the things I've found most inspiring is to know I can always begin again. No matter how many times I may have been swept up in a painful emotion, difficult mind state, or unwise behavior, freedom is always available—in this moment, this breath, here, right now.

It's with this spirit that I encourage you to engage with the practices in this book, as well as with the supplementary audio recordings and other content available for free at this book's website, http://www.newharbinger.com/44086 (see the back of this book for detailed access instructions). I look forward to accompanying you on this journey.

CHAPTER 1

Training Our Mind to Transform Our Habits

There is no need to struggle to be free; the absence of struggle is itself freedom.

—Chögyam Trungpa Rinpoche

The message of this book is simple and direct: You can change your life. You can live with greater purpose, peace, and freedom.

The path is an ancient one, confirmed by the most recent findings of neuroscience and psychology: through the power of awareness—by bringing mindfulness to your present-moment experience—you can train yourself to let go of habits of thought, word, and action that cause harm and suffering. And you can develop and nurture habits that lead to well-being and happiness.

Much of our suffering and dissatisfaction come from *habits*, behaviors and patterns of thinking that become automatic and unconscious through repetition. Habits can be healthy (such as putting on a seatbelt when getting in a car, or brushing one's teeth after meals) or unhealthy (such as spending excessive amounts of time online, or eating or drinking in unconscious or harmful ways). Changing our habits—cultivating healthy ones and letting go of more harmful ones—is a key to living with greater happiness and ease.

Everyone wants to be happy, as the Dalai Lama often says. We don't come into the world and grow up wanting to be sad, depressed, dejected, or dissatisfied. The conditions of our life—difficult or more comfortable—can play a role in contributing to our sense of well-being. But almost all of us act in ways that lead to dissatisfaction and suffering, such as making choices that do not serve or benefit us, even though that is not what we are seeking. Or we fail to do things that would support our health and well-being—such as exercising regularly, getting enough sleep, or eating healthfully—despite seeing their benefits.

Can you think of any of your own behaviors or patterns of thinking that are harmful, unhealthy, or not how you want to live? Let's dig a little deeper with the following questions:

- Do you judge yourself harshly when you fail to live up to your own standards?

- Do you eat or drink in unconscious ways and regret it later?

- Do you consistently put off tasks that you know you need to take care of?

- Do you find yourself getting angry or irritated by family members, friends, or work colleagues when they do or say something that rubs you the wrong way?

- Do you spend a lot of time feeling stressed or anxious about things that you have to do?

- Do you spend too much time checking devices, surfing the Internet, or posting or sharing on social media?

- Do you wish you would exercise more, get adequate sleep, meditate, or include other healthy practices into your daily routine?

Most of us probably would say yes to one or more of these questions.

Still, even when we recognize and identify unhealthy or unhelpful behaviors—or healthy ones we wish we did more of—habits, once set in motion, can be difficult to change. And we can then feel frustrated, disappointed, or unhappy that we don't seem to be able to change our behavior.

The good news is that we can change unhealthy behaviors and cultivate beneficial habits and patterns of thinking that support our well-being. Here are the key steps to changing habits and enhancing well-being:

1. *Understanding why and how we get stuck*, particularly the role of evolutionary brain processes in forming habits that can be hard to change

2. *Recognizing the possibility of training our mind* and the liberating power of mindful awareness in making change in our life

3. *Engaging in a path of practice*—centered on mindful acceptance of our experience as it is—to let go of unhealthy behaviors and nourish and develop more helpful ones

In this book, you'll learn how to work with these steps to change unhealthy habits and engage in helpful ones. First, though, it helps to understand how we get stuck with unhealthy habits in the first place.

Why and How We Get Stuck

The brain and nervous system we've inherited from millions of years of evolution are a wonder and give us much to be thankful for. We are here because our ancestors survived through difficult and dangerous times, and succeeded in passing on their genes to the next generation.

But as Robert Sapolsky, Rick Hanson, Daniel Kahneman, and others have shown, the way we have evolved—and particularly the brain and its processes passed down through thousands of generations of evolution—can get us into trouble.

A zebra that survives being pursued by a lion is able, after a period of recovery, to go back to grazing without any post-traumatic stress. We humans, after surviving a dangerous or threatening experience, are much more likely to revisit and replay the memory—and continue to suffer as a result. The zebra is dealing with the present-moment threat when it arises and can shake out the stress and tension when it passes. We humans, with our capacity for thinking and reflection, can keep revisiting the past and reliving the experience, often giving rise to unhealthy responses to alleviate the unpleasant feelings (Sapolsky 2004).

Additionally, because it was more important for our ancestors to escape life-threatening situations than to have positive experiences (eating, mating, and so forth), which could wait until the threat had passed, evolution has primed our species to focus more attention on negative experiences than on positive ones.

As Hanson (2009) has said, we are "like Velcro for negative experiences and Teflon for positive ones." Our focus on the negative means we typically fail to take advantage of and internalize positive experiences, and often overreact to negative ones. And to avoid negative experiences or feelings, we often develop unhealthy habits that cause us suffering.

Moreover, as I discuss in my book *The Here-and-Now Habit* (Byrne 2016), our human brain has evolved two, at times competing, brain systems. The first is an instinctual and automatic mode of response, with origins in threats to survival and linked to more ancient brain processes. The second is a slower and reflective mode associated with our more advanced brain areas of the prefrontal cortex and with more deliberate and rational thinking.

The conflict between these two brain systems can lead us to outcomes that are not in our interest. An example is when unhealthy habits develop to satisfy short-term needs for comfort and perceived safety, but become difficult to change and cause harm in the longer term.

The automatic brain processes that have evolved to help us survive are essential when we need to respond immediately to a threat (for example, jumping out of the way of something moving quickly toward us). But when these automatic processes are activated over an extended period (for example, by repeated anxious thinking about how we are going to be able to get a school paper or report written by the deadline), we can experience significant suffering.

We'll discuss other factors that lead us to make choices that don't benefit us in the long term and that can be difficult to change. But the good news is that we can change even long-entrenched unhealthy habits. We can train our minds and live with greater happiness and freedom.

We Can Train Our Mind

Many philosophies and wisdom traditions have long held that our happiness and peace is not a function of our birth, wealth, or circumstances but of how we meet our experience—how we respond to the conditions that life presents.

We're all familiar with stories of deeply unhappy millionaires as well as people living with joy and peace in harsh conditions. Today we are seeing a convergence in understanding between ancient Buddhist and other wisdom teachings, and the findings of modern neuroscience and psychology on the sources of happiness. Each sees our happiness and well-being as, to a considerable extent, being an "inside job"—a product of the attitudes with which we meet our experience.

Buddhist teachings are grounded in the understanding that peace is possible in any moment—if we meet what is here now (for example, restlessness, difficult news, tiredness, joy, physical discomfort or pain, excitement, frustration, ease) with acceptance and genuine kindness. This potential is not something to be believed as an act of faith but rather can be tested in our own experience.

Our happiness and peace depend on how we meet this moment, and on the qualities we choose to cultivate from moment to moment. We can think of it as like planting seeds: If we plant seeds of kindness, gratitude, generosity, or compassion, our mind will be increasingly inclined toward the peace and joy that accompanies these mind states. If we think angry thoughts that fuel further hostile thoughts and actions, this tendency or pattern will lead to a predominantly conflictive or hostile quality of mind.

This is the Buddhist understanding of *karma*: our intentions—and the words and acts that arise from them—create the conditions for our future well-being or suffering. In the present moment we sow the seeds of our future happiness or dissatisfaction. What we repeatedly do, we become.

The key to transforming our mind and our life is to meet this moment with mindfulness, so that we can choose what we do and become. Bringing mindful awareness to any aspect of our experience—bodily sensations, the feeling tone of our experience, emotions, mind states, our inner or outer environment—is a doorway to insight and freedom.

The practice of mindfulness is crucial to the two practices the Buddha provided as a path to complete freedom in our lives:

- *Abandon the unskillful.* Bring attention to whatever you are experiencing, meet what's present with openhearted awareness, and cultivate a practice of letting go of any patterns of holding (such as clinging, resistance, spacing out).

- *Cultivate the good.* Develop and nurture mind states of ease, nonclinging, gratitude, compassion, generosity, joy, and other wholesome states that are conducive to well-being and freedom.

When you abandon mind states, thoughts, and actions that lead to suffering—and develop and nurture those that lead to happiness—you are on a path to true freedom of the heart.

The skills and practices that you will discover in this book will show you how to let go of unhealthy habits and develop more beneficial ones—with the objective of living more happily, peacefully, and freely. They are practices to help you dance with life rather than being in an incessant struggle with it and with your experience.

This ancient approach to deepening freedom and peace that has been practiced for more than a hundred generations is now in dialogue with modern psychology and neuroscience, which are reaching similar conclusions about the potential for cultivating happiness and well-being.

Recent Research in Neuroscience and Psychology

One of the most important developments in brain research during the past two decades is the realization that our brain changes throughout our lives, rather than ceasing to develop further once we reach adulthood. Neuroscientific studies now show that what we do and how we use our attention bring changes to our brain and can radically affect the quality of our life.

Neuroplasticity, or our brain's ability to change, has been demonstrated in studies of musicians, London taxi drivers, meditators, and others (Maguire, Woollett, and Spiers 2006).

Research on the impacts of meditation has shown changes in the brains of meditators associated with practice over short periods. A 2011 study comparing meditators in an eight-week mindfulness program with a control group showed an increase in the density of neurons in brain areas associated with self-awareness, compassion, and introspection, plus a decrease in density in brain areas associated with stress and anxiety among the meditators. The changes were linked to an average of twenty-seven minutes of meditation a day over an eight-week period. Similar changes were not found in the control group (Hölzel et al. 2011).

Broader studies also demonstrate that our happiness is not just a product of our genes—the idea that we are born a happy person or are not—or our circumstances. Rather, studies by Sonja Lyubomirsky and colleagues point to a significant proportion of our happiness depending on our intentional activity.

Lyubomirsky concludes that 50 percent of the difference among people's happiness levels can be accounted for by their genetically determined set points. Only 10 percent of the variance in happiness levels is explained by a person's life circumstances or situations. And, significantly, 40 percent is within our ability to control—and can be increased or decreased through what we do in our daily lives and how we think (Lyubomirsky 2007).

Other studies that explored the impact of cultivating practices of *loving-kindness* (Byrne 2016), *self-compassion* (Byrne 2016), and *gratitude* (Emmons 2013) on emotional and psychological well-being showed significant improvements arising through training in these practices. As Richard O'Connor argues in his book *Rewire*, "With enough deliberate practice, we can rewire ourselves" (2014, 28).

A Path of Practice to Change Habits

Scientific research confirms that we can train our minds and effect changes in our brains through the actions we take and the practices we cultivate. But habits take time and effort to establish and, once established, they can be difficult to change. That is because they are off the radar screen of our awareness: through repetition they have become automatic and unconscious. This makes having a path of training for changing them particularly important and necessary.

Mindfulness is an ideal path of training for changing habits because, by its nature, it brings into awareness what has become unconscious—making what is invisible visible. We are then in a position to make more healthy choices—to let go of habits that don't serve us and to cultivate others that are of benefit.

Some of the ways in which mindfulness supports habit change are:

- Identifying behaviors that cause us harm and others that enhance our life

- Helping us cultivate strong intentions to make change, which is essential in developing new habits and letting go of unhelpful ones

- Cultivating appropriate attitudes—acceptance, self-compassion, curiosity, patience, and others—that help nourish the soil for effective habit change

- Developing skills—such as focus, concentration, and wise effort—that can help in changing habits

Mindfulness is a *radical* approach to habit change in that it addresses the *roots* of a behavior rather than just the external *expressions*. It helps us to address the feelings, impulses, and triggers that underlie the behavior, such as a bodily craving that moves us toward eating a sweet to feel relief, or a feeling of discomfort or anxiety that habitually leads us to check our email or Facebook account. These are unpleasant feelings; because we do not want to open to them, we find (often unhealthy) habits to help us escape them. Mindfulness invites us to open to and experience directly the energies (feelings, impulses, and sensations moving in us) that drive us toward and keep us stuck in unhealthy or unwanted behaviors.

When we train ourselves to experience the underlying energies with acceptance and genuine kindness—normalizing and not resisting what we are feeling—we are less prone to default to habitual responses. We can learn to stay with difficult sensations, feelings, and thoughts, as well as the feelings of resistance that can manifest in habits of getting angry and judgmental toward ourselves or others. We can come to see that these energies don't stay forever and that we can choose not to act out the unhealthy habit.

Or we can substitute a healthy behavior for a less beneficial response. As a result, our unhealthy habits can fall into disuse or be replaced with healthier ones. Healthy habits enhance our life; unhealthy habits limit our possibilities and our freedom. An important additional benefit of addressing the roots of the habit rather than simply the behavior is that we are less prone to replace one unhealthy habit with another one (for example, giving up smoking and then eating large amounts of sweets).

Replacing Unhealthy Habits with Healthy Ones

Research shows that an approach to habit change that couples the breaking of existing unhealthy habits with the development of healthy ones produces the most long-term beneficial results (Wood and Neal 2016). As O'Connor notes, "We have to learn new habits to replace our old self-destructive patterns, and as we learn them, new channels in our brain become stronger and deeper" (2014, 242).

This two-pronged approach of habit-swapping is utilized here, pairing the letting go of an unhealthy habit with the cultivation of a healthy habit. We begin by getting to the roots of unhealthy habits, working with the energies of:

- **Wanting or craving**—and cultivating *acceptance, gratitude, and kindness*

- **Self-judgment, anger, aversion**—and cultivating *self-compassion and loving-kindness*

- **Distraction, daydreaming, spacing out**—and cultivating *attention and concentration*

- **Worry, anxiety, and rumination**—and cultivating *joy and contentment*

From there, we'll explore ways of untangling ourselves from unhealthy habitual behaviors that can emerge from these energies and cultivating helpful ones:

- **Unhealthy consuming**, including eating, drinking, smoking, drug-taking, shopping—and cultivating habits of *healthy living*, such as movement or activity, supportive food choices, adequate sleep, or meditation

- **Online escapism**, including cell phone, Internet, texting, and TV bingeing—and cultivating *wise intention and conscious action*

- **Angry, harmful, or unkind speech**—and cultivating habits of *mindful communication*

- **Habits of doing, busyness, living on autopilot**—and cultivating habits of *mindfulness in daily life*

- **Unconscious behaviors that create unhappiness**—and developing *curiosity and interest* in our experience

It all begins with the development of a regular meditation practice (or deepening your practice, if you already have one) and learning skills to cultivate mindfulness in daily life.

Let's begin this practice to align your thoughts and actions with your deepest values and intentions so that you can live a happier, healthier, and freer life.

CHAPTER 2

The Powers of Habits and Mindfulness

What is not brought to consciousness comes to us as fate.

—C. G. Jung

One evening, a friend, Matthew, asked if he could talk with me about his drinking. He'd grown up in a culture where drinking alcohol accompanied almost every experience and life situation. He shared that he drank to have fun, find romance, drown the sorrows of his team losing—and celebrate their victories—and make life more bearable... And once a drinking session began, Matthew would continue until the evening finished or the establishment closed.

As he got older, he saw that this habit was no longer working for him. The day after an evening's drinking, he tended to feel low energy and unfocused, and he sensed that alcohol fueled many of his relationships but prevented them from going deeper. He didn't view himself as an alcoholic—he was able to give it a break for a week or a month at a time. He also carried on a productive working life, and his partner shared a similar lifestyle. But much of his life revolved around drinking, and it was hard for him to imagine what his life would look like if he didn't drink.

Matthew was smart enough to know that his drinking wasn't making him happy, that once he went out with his friends, the drinking habit was in the driver's seat rather than him. He knew that it would take effort and perseverance to turn his life in a healthier direction. He knew too about 12-step programs and other forms of support available. The stumbling block was determining if he had the will and perseverance to make a change, and if "the game was worth the candle," or whether he was willing to pay the price.

You likely face the same choice Matthew did when it comes to your unhealthy habits. In this chapter we'll explore the power of established habits and the power of mindfulness to move you in new directions. We'll discuss what habits are, how they form, why they can be difficult to change, as well as the important role that mindfulness can play in changing unhealthy habits and cultivating more beneficial ones.

I'll then invite you to explore the circumstances, conditions, and choices that brought you to where you are in your life—and to determine what is calling for your attention—so that you might live a life of freedom and joy.

Habits and Their Evolutionary Role

A habit typically begins as a conscious, intentional act designed to achieve a goal or reward. With consistent repetition in similar contexts, the brain makes the original intentional behavior *automatic* and *unconscious*—and subject to different brain processes.

Ultimately, any behavior or pattern of thought that we repeat often enough can become habitual. And unless we intentionally break the pattern, it usually stays that way. As Charles Duhigg, best-selling author of *The Power of Habit*, notes: "When a habit emerges, the brain stops fully participating in decision making. It stops working so hard, or diverts focus to other tasks. So unless you deliberately *fight* a habit—unless you find new routines—the pattern will unfold automatically" (2012, 20).

Habit formation played a critical role in human evolution. Making intentional behaviors automatic (taking the same path in search of food when it had led to success in the past, for example) allowed the human brain to conserve energy and be more efficient. It also opened up space for creativity and invention. When brain power doesn't need to be used to work out how to walk across the room or relearn how to ride a bicycle each time we get on it, we can devote mental energy to going to the moon, inventing the electric light, or painting the Sistine Chapel.

Why Habits Are Difficult to Change

When a behavior is repeated often enough under consistent conditions it becomes automatic and is assigned to instinctual—rather than intentional—brain operations. The Nobel Prize–winning psychologist Daniel Kahneman called this mode of cognitive function "System 1." System 1's operations, he notes, are "often emotionally charged; they are also governed by habit and are therefore difficult to control or modify." He distinguished these from the intentional operations of "System 2," which are "more likely to be consciously monitored and deliberately controlled; they are also relatively flexible" (2011, 698).

Walter Mischel, renowned for his experiments into children's ability to defer gratification and author of *The Marshmallow Test* (2014), called these two different brain processes the *hot emotional system* and the *cool cognitive system*. Think of the way a marshmallow or other tasty treat might be more compelling to a child (or adult) than the *thought* that they could have two of these later if they waited and cooled their craving.

When habitual behaviors that are faster acting and linked to more-ancient survival responses come into conflict with intentions that are slower, more deliberate, and associated with the more recently developed brain, the habitual behaviors tend to win out.

Research studies show that as habit strength increases, intentions play less of a role in predicting behavior: "Habits yield tunnel vision, thus reducing the effectiveness of interventions aimed at changing behavior through conscious cognitive deliberation" (Nilsen et al. 2012, 2).

This is not a problem where healthy and desired behaviors (such as exercising, eating healthfully, or living according to our values and intentions) are concerned. But when we develop unhealthy habits (such as spending excessive time online, procrastinating, worrying, or eating or drinking unconsciously), the "stickiness" of habits can be a significant problem.

We can all think of times when we identified a behavior as one we wanted to change and resolved to embark on a more healthy course, only to find ourselves gravitating back to the old behavior—often under stress or other pressure. Intentions are necessary but often not sufficient. This is where mindfulness comes in.

Mindfulness Makes the Unconscious Conscious

Mindfulness—meeting present-moment experience with acceptance and without judgment—is a key to changing and developing habits. Mindfulness brings behaviors and patterns of thinking that have become automatic and unconscious into the light of awareness—it *makes the unconscious conscious*.

Mindfulness allows us to get to the *roots* of unhealthy habits so that we can work with the underlying *habit energies*—wanting or craving, resisting experience, checking out, or busyness—rather than just addressing the external behaviors. We can then choose to make changes that support greater well-being. And we are less likely to replace one unhealthy habit with another.

Here are some of the main ways in which mindfulness can help us abandon unhealthy habits and cultivate more beneficial ones:

Mindfulness can prevent an unhealthy urge from arising. By bringing the habit pattern into awareness, it is possible to notice the habit *before* it has been expressed or acted on— and then choose a healthier course. For example, by taking another route home, rather than walking past the shop where we regularly stop for a jelly doughnut, we can stop the habit before it has a chance to start.

Mindfulness can teach us how to "ride the wave." When we notice we are in the middle of an unwanted habit, we can learn, through practice, to ride the waves of challenging urges, feelings, and emotions rather than acting them out. For example, we can stay with some tension in our body and anxious thoughts rather than having a cigarette or checking our likes on Facebook. With a mindfulness practice, we can come back and learn to find peace in the present moment, just as it is. We are able to choose a more healthy alternative response.

Mindfulness nurtures self-compassion. After a habit event, we can meet "lapses" with compassion rather than beating ourselves up, while renewing our commitment to a new, helpful behavior.

Mindfulness helps us set intentions. Our intentions connect us with what matters most and help us identify what gets in the way of living freely and with ease. Mindfulness helps us clarify and cultivate strong and clear intentions, to develop new behaviors or abandon habits that don't serve us.

Mindfulness builds our capacity to focus attention. It helps us learn to open to and stay with uncomfortable feelings and difficult urges and emotions without escaping into familiar habit patterns. More than a century ago, William James called the training of this capacity to pay attention and bring back a wandering mind "an education par excellence" (James 1890). The renowned researcher of "flow" states, Mihaly Csikszentmihalyi describes attention as "psychic energy" that is critical for determining the shape and content of our lives (1990, 33). Mindfulness helps us build the muscle of attention that is an essential faculty in working with the automatic and unconscious qualities of habits as well as the contexts, urges, and triggers that set habits in motion.

Mindfulness invites acceptance. This means we begin where we are, acknowledging the truth of our situation or experience, however difficult it might be. It is only by beginning where we are that we can hope to bring meaningful change to our habits and our lives.

Mindfulness embodies kindness. With kindness we open space for our experience to be as it is—not judging, resisting, or trying to hold on to particular feelings or states. When we meet our experience in a kind manner, we can allow the habit energies to come and go without needing to act on them.

Mindfulness encourages curiosity. With curiosity we shift from being swept up in a strong feeling, emotion, or habit energy to being aware of the feelings and urges. We are then able to observe them come and go without acting on them.

A variety of mindfulness skills and practices can support us in letting go of unhelpful habits and developing more beneficial ones:

- Using the breath, bodily sensations, sounds, or other focus as a *home base* or *anchor* for our attention, and bringing attention back when the mind moves into discursive thought

- Riding the waves of difficult emotions, urges, or mind states—and seeing that they don't last forever but come and go in their own time when met with acceptance and kindness

- Investigating the underlying beliefs that often keep us tied to unhealthy habits, and learning to free ourselves from them when they no longer serve us

We can also cultivate beneficial qualities (for example, gratitude, self-compassion, loving-kindness, equanimity, and joy) that provide antidotes to worry, self-judgment, anger, and other painful emotions and mind states, allowing us to let go of unhealthy habits and develop more beneficial ones.

Cultivating Mindfulness Skills to Change Habits

If you have an unhealthy habit that you wish to change, there is no need to resist it or in some way rid yourself of it. The essence of mindfulness practice lies in seeing things as they are and recognizing that if we do not try to hold on to experiences or resist them, the experiences come and go on their own. They "self-liberate," in an expression used in Tibetan Buddhism. We can see how this process operates in relation to different kinds of *habit energies*.

When you become aware of the energy of *wanting* or *craving* something—an energy of reaching out for the desired object—you can pause and experience the feelings in the body and mind (such as tightness, grasping, or thoughts of wanting or needing), and let them come and go with acceptance and kindness. You can also invite in more beneficial mind states, such as gratitude and acceptance.

When you experience the energy of *aversion* or *resistance*—expressed in anger, judgment, impatience, annoyance, fear, or other feeling or emotion—you can bring awareness to these energies and let them come and go, riding the waves of difficult sensations and emotions. You can also cultivate self-compassion or loving-kindness, a quality of friendliness and care that we can develop to ourselves and others, as an antidote to the difficult or contracted feelings.

If you feel the energy of *distraction*, or wanting to escape or check out from your current experience (for example, by going online or engaging in other electronic activity), you can invite yourself to stay with the underlying feelings, letting them come and go without spacing out, and coming back to the body or breath when your attention wanders. You can also cultivate attention and focus, and find pleasure in the present moment by bringing awareness to the breath or other object.

When the energy of *worry*, *anxiety*, or *busyness* arises, you can train yourself to stay with these feelings, noting how they feel in the body, bringing awareness to your thoughts, and letting them come and go. You can also cultivate contentment and joy, inviting the arising of calm and contentment in the present moment, and deepening joy in your aliveness.

When It Feels Like Too Much

In presenting these skills and practices of mindfulness to help us change entrenched habits, it is important to acknowledge that it is not a simple or easy process—and that it can be difficult to stay with difficult emotions, feelings, sensations, or thoughts. Many of us come to these practices with a history of trauma, intense stress, or chronic pain. As much as we might have the intention and desire to be with the difficult states, our brain may be vehemently telling us, "No, I can't stay" or "This is too much." And we can end up feeling as if we have failed or as if the practice has failed us.

Rather than thinking we have to grit our way through painful or difficult feelings, we can cultivate skills to help us open to and free ourselves from these painful experiences in a more gradual way. A first step is to connect with *resources* that are available to us. A resource in psychology can be any feeling, sensation, memory, relationship, or experience that allows us to feel safe, grounded, peaceful, or other positive quality. And this resource can help us come back into balance when we are feeling activated, overwhelmed, or otherwise unable to tolerate our experience.

You might take some time now to think about your own resources: a pleasant and peaceful bodily feeling, your own breathing, the thought of someone in your life who loves or loved you unconditionally, God, a spiritual figure, a dear friend, a special place where you feel peaceful and at ease... When working with the practices in this book, come back to one or more of these resources if you feel overwhelmed or as if things are too much.

You can also experiment with moving back and forth between a difficult feeling or experience and the resource, staying as long and as fully as you can with the difficult feeling and moving to your resource if the feelings become too intense. Then, stay with the resource until you have come back into balance. And when you feel ready, return your attention to the place of activation. This gradual moving back and forth is termed *pendulation*, and staying for a limited period of time with the feelings of activation is known as *titration* in Somatic Experiencing, a mind-body approach to healing trauma developed by Peter Levine (1997).

Starting the Process of Change

We have been talking about mindfulness and meditation a lot up to this point. Now it's time to practice it! Please find a supportive environment where you will not be disturbed for fifteen to thirty minutes and take a comfortable seat. I'll be inviting you to journal answers to questions in the second part of this exercise, so you might find it helpful to have pen and paper near at hand.

Mindful Reflection

Take some time to reflect on where you are in your life, wherever you happen to be. Think about the factors that helped shape your life and the choices you made.

Think about your ancestors, where they came from, their journeys, their struggles, challenges, and hopes... Your family, your parents, caregivers, siblings, and other family members... How your family situation helped shape your life, the hardships, the privileges and blessings, the challenges and pains... How your family and upbringing opened up possibilities in some areas and limited others, how they affected the choices you made...

Think about your community, religion, or other influences... Your schooling, friends, the jobs and work you've done... The wider culture... How these all affected your life and your choices...

Think about your health... Your financial situation... The things that happened to you, the joys and sorrows...

And think about the choices you made in response to both external and internal conditions, about what happened to you and your hopes and fears... Think about how some of the choices you made and the beliefs you developed about the world and your place in it may have led to outcomes that you feel good about (for example, trusting in yourself and the kindness of others, or developing a sense of acceptance of yourself)... And think about how other choices, perhaps affected by fear or what felt possible at the time, led to outcomes or habits that don't help you now and leave you feeling disconnected, guilty, unhappy, or stuck...

In an openhearted way—without regret, blame, or judgment—hold all that has come up with kindness and acceptance. Take some time to reflect on where you are now... Notice any insights, lessons, or learning that comes to you as you think about all these factors and experiences that helped create the conditions for who and where you are today...

Wherever you are in your life is where you are right now. Any change has to begin from here, from a deep-rooted acceptance of where you are today, where you are right now. If you are flying high, you can enjoy the flight and remember the truth that everything changes. If you are at rock bottom, know that recognizing and accepting this truth is the prerequisite for moving toward a more hopeful and fulfilling life.

And as you sit with what has arisen, you might ask yourself, *What do I plan to do with this one life I have?*

As you reflect on your life as it is right now, ask yourself, *What do I care about and value most deeply? What matters most to me?* Touch into your deepest wish for yourself and your life... It might come to you as a word (peace, joy, love, ease, creativity, kindness) or as an image of yourself living according to your deepest wishes and aspirations... Allow yourself to experience whatever comes up in your body, emotions, mind... Sit with this aspiration and any feelings that come up...

Now, shifting from the meditative reflection into journaling, you might write down thoughts that come to you as you respond to the following questions:

- What gets in the way of living according to this intention or wish for myself?

- What prevents me from living with ease, peace, joy, or other expression of well-being?

- Is there a specific behavior or a pattern of thinking that leaves me feeling unhappy, stressed, anxious, judgmental, or other emotion (for example, putting off things that need to get done, being distracted, being unfocused much of the time, spending large swaths of time online, eating or drinking unconsciously, worrying, stressing out, getting activated by the political situation)?

- Is there something that I'd like to be doing that I'm not doing (such as exercising, eating consciously, or developing skills)?

Let yourself take in whatever comes up—in your body, emotions, mind...

Now ask yourself two more questions:

- How important is it to me to make change in this area?

- What would this change look like?

Begin, if you can, by identifying one area that you wish to bring mindfulness to, in order to effect a positive change.

In the chapters that follow, you'll have the opportunity to bring mindfulness to this (or another) specific habit. You will be supported by skills and practices that will help you let go of an unhealthy habit or develop a more beneficial one. You'll also learn other skills to abandon habits that don't serve you and develop qualities—such as gratitude, compassion, joy, and acceptance—that are powerfully associated with increased well-being and happiness. We'll begin in the next chapter with the bedrock habit of cultivating or deepening a regular meditation practice and bringing mindfulness into daily life.

CHAPTER 3

Developing a Bedrock Meditation Habit

We've discussed how we can choose the way we respond to our experience to change our lives and live with greater freedom and happiness. We highlighted the importance of mindfulness in working to let go of unhealthy or unwanted habits, and in cultivating more beneficial ones, by bringing awareness to behaviors and patterns of thinking that have become automatic and unconscious. And we worked to set an intention for our mindfulness practice and our habit change.

In this chapter, we discuss how to cultivate *bedrock habits*—habits that can support us in addressing other habits in our lives—starting with two skills: mindfulness in daily life and as a regular meditation practice. We also explore skills and practices of awareness that help us abandon unwanted habits and develop more helpful ones.

When we are not consciously cultivating awareness, we easily gravitate toward what feels compelling in the moment or what will move us away from a feeling of discomfort or unease. But when we deepen the practice of awareness of our present-moment experience, we counter the habitual tendency of the mind to default to distraction and checking out.

Two readily available ways to hone our awareness are to:

- Bring mindfulness into the activities of daily life, and

- Take time out of our everyday activities for the formal practice of meditation.

We'll discuss each of these areas and provide tools to incorporate them into daily life.

Formal and Informal Practices

Ultimately, every moment is a moment to be here, present for our experience, allowing what is present to come and go in its own time. Or it's a moment to be somewhere else, lost in thought, wanting something we don't currently have, or caught up in a habitual behavior. Ultimately, no moment is more important than any other moment—sitting in meditation is not better than walking in the woods or brushing our teeth. What matters is the quality of our presence: *Am I here, aware, open to my experience? Or lost in planning, craving, worrying, or ruminating?*

It can be helpful, however, to distinguish between times we set aside specifically to practice mindfulness—typically in sitting or other forms of meditation—and times we bring mindfulness to our daily activities. It can be useful to think of the intentionally scheduled meditation periods as *formal* practice, and the times we bring awareness to everyday life as *informal* practice.

Formal and informal practices are mutually supportive and are each an essential part of mindfulness training. The formal period of meditation can typically give us a more extended time relatively free from external distractions to cultivate moment-to-moment awareness. The more we deepen our formal practice, the more inner capacity we develop to bring mindfulness into other areas of our life. When we are cultivating mindfulness informally in daily life, we are also strengthening our capacity to be present. We create supportive conditions that lead to a calmer and more focused mind when we sit down for formal meditation practice.

Since most of us spend the majority of our waking hours outside of formal meditation, let's begin cultivating our capacities to be mindfully present by looking at ways we can cultivate mindfulness in daily life, exploring how this helps us develop healthy habits and let go of unhelpful ones.

Informal Practice: Mindfulness in Daily Life

There are many ways we can harness the activities of our daily life and observe our minds to deepen mindfulness. The following skills and practices are accessible—with any appropriate adaptations—for everyone.

Bringing Mindfulness to Everyday Activities

Take an activity you do every day or regularly, and consciously bring mindfulness to it. As you deepen your capacity to be present for your experience, you can practice mindfully engaging with just about any task. Here are some examples:

- If you are washing dishes, allow yourself to feel the water and suds on your hands, experiencing the sensations and temperature of the water... Stay present for *this* dish and come back when the mind moves into thought.

- At work, if you walk a short distance to the restroom try taking that period as a conscious time to practice mindfulness: Let your attention come out of thinking and bring awareness to your body as you walk. Check in with how you are feeling (tense, preoccupied, or relaxed, for example) and let the walk to and from the restroom be a period of coming back to yourself and the present moment.

- If you drive to work, consciously commit to being as fully present as you can while you are behind the wheel: feeling your body on the seat, being aware of your environment, coming back to your body and breath when you move into automatic pilot.

Taking a Mindful Pause

An informal practice that you can engage in at different times during the day, the *mindful pause* helps you reconnect with the present moment. When you are caught up in striving, obsessing, or leaning into the future, pausing helps you to reconnect with the vitality only available here and now. You can experiment with bringing these practices into the flow of your daily activities.

- *The three-breath break:* When you become aware that you've been focusing on an activity for an extended period, or are transitioning between activities, take a three-breath break. Let's try it right now: Pause, closing your eyes if possible, and take a deep breath intentionally into the belly. Allow the abdomen to expand. Then let the exhalation be longer than the in-breath. Relax and release any places of tightness or tension in the body with each exhalation, such as around the face, neck, and shoulders. Repeat twice more.

- *The telephone ring as a mindfulness bell:* When the telephone rings, take a few seconds to use the sound to bring yourself fully into your body. You can feel your feet squarely on the floor as you walk over to the phone. Relax any muscles that may be contracted, especially in the face, mouth, and jaw. Inhale and exhale more deeply for a breath or two, then answer the call.

- *A stoplight as a signal for a mindful pause:* When driving (or walking in an area with pedestrian signals), use the occasion of each red stoplight as an opportunity for pausing. Depending on the situation, you can use the moment to breathe more deeply and release any places of tension or contraction in the body.

- *A mindful pause in goal-oriented activities:* When you are involved in a goal-oriented activity (such as reading, working at a computer, cleaning, or planning), begin by pausing, sitting comfortably, and allowing your eyes to close. Take a few deep breaths, and with each exhalation let go of any worries or thoughts about what you are going to do next. Soften and invite a releasing of any

tightness in the body. Notice what you are experiencing as you inhabit the pause. What sensations are you aware of in your body? Do you feel
anxious or restless as you step out of your mental
stories? Do you feel pulled to resume your activity? Can you allow, for this moment, whatever is
happening inside?

Whenever you feel stuck or disconnected, invite yourself
to begin fresh in the moment by pausing, relaxing, and
paying attention to your immediate experience.

Bringing Mindfulness to Daily Habits

It is the nature of habits, as we've discussed, to go off the
radar screen once they are established; they're governed by
different brain processes than our conscious, intentional
acts. So a key step in changing behaviors that are not helpful
is to bring them into awareness so that we can see the costs
and envision possible alternative behaviors. We do this by
bringing mindfulness to times when we are feeling discomfort, unease, tension, dissatisfaction, or suffering. These feelings will often be a signal to help us identify habitual ways in
which we avoid or move away from difficult feelings. Here
are some examples:

- You feel anxious or unfocused with an unpleasant bodily feeling of tension or craving. Your

mind moves habitually to eating something sweet to provide comfort or fill an emotional gap. Pause. Try bringing awareness to the difficult or unpleasant feeling. Allow yourself to feel it and ask yourself, *What would be a healthy way of responding to this feeling that would allow me to feel good about myself and my choices?* You might decide to take a walk or eat a healthy snack. You might choose to reflect on things that you are grateful for in your life.

• You're in a work meeting and feeling bored. Your thoughts go to how people are repeating themselves, how the issue being discussed is of little import, how you wish you were somewhere else. You mentally check out from the meeting and start reading your email and social media posts on your phone. Instead, when you become aware of feeling bored, bring attention to your bodily feelings—letting them come and go—and observe your thoughts without proliferating them. Consciously commit to bringing your attention back to the meeting. You might reflect that your colleagues are doing their best and think about a contribution you might offer that could focus the meeting on its objectives.

Cultivating Mindful Mini Habits

An excellent way of developing new healthier habits is to take small steps—cultivating mindful mini habits that lay the basis for meaningful changes in our life. What is powerful about mini habits is that they do not take a high expenditure of energy or effort to accomplish. Think about working five minutes a day on a project you have been putting off, or writing fifty or one hundred words a day if you wish to finish a report, book, or writing assignment.

As well as not taking major effort, mini habits prime the brain to engage in the activity on a regular basis and allow us to do more than the minimum—if we choose—but without putting pressure or expectations on ourselves. It is the initial effort that typically takes energy and willpower, and that can be a stumbling block, particularly if we are asking ourselves to run three miles rather than to run for three minutes.

Some mini habits that I began while writing this book include: working on my taxes for five minutes a day, since this is a task that I have found easy to put off; spending five minutes a day cleaning my office, which can get cluttered; and giving away or recycling one item a day to lessen the amount of unused clothing and other household materials.

To help exercise your habit-formation muscles, consider starting two to three mini habits and commit to writing them down, doing them on a daily basis, and checking off each day when you have accomplished them. Notice if you feel inclined to do more than the basic commitment but without any expectations or judgment. Notice if the mini habit has become easier or more automatic.

Formal Practice: Meditation as a Bedrock Habit

The formal practice of meditation can operate as a bedrock habit. Meditation can provide skills to let go of habits that do not serve us and to develop those that provide benefit in our lives.

As we've seen, meditation helps us develop and change habits by strengthening our power of attention, by giving us an opportunity to work with habits as they arise in meditation, and by helping us cultivate qualities (such as curiosity, self-acceptance, and compassion) that can help us transform habit patterns. Meditation also provides us with an opportunity to clarify our *intentions* to abandon or develop a habit, along with a time to *review* and take stock of how we are working with habits.

Some keys to cultivating a daily or regular meditation practice are:

- **Connect with your intention.** To develop a regular practice, reflect on the extent of your commitment, the advantages and benefits it can bring to your life, and how to overcome obstacles to developing a daily practice.

- **Ensure regularity.** Try to meditate at the same time and the same place each day, if possible; this helps the brain make the practice into a positive habit. Start by making a commitment to sit daily for a set period of time—ten, fifteen, or thirty minutes—for ten days using the Ten-Day Mindfulness Meditation for Habit Change practice outlined in this chapter (in abridged form) and online (in its entirety in both written and audio form at http://newhar binger.com/44086). Check off each day that you sit. If you miss a day, make an extra effort to ensure that you sit for meditation the following days.

- **Reflect.** When you have finished the ten-day period, reflect on how your practice has been. Identify areas where you might want to focus attention, for example, cultivating particular practices or qualities of mind such as kindness, curiosity, attention, and so forth. Make a commitment for another period. Continue until the practice becomes a habit.

- **Find a meditation buddy.** Choose someone who is also committed to developing a practice or wishes to sit regularly. Sit together or share with each other how your practice is progressing.

- **Turn to your resources.** As we noted in the previous chapter, it's helpful to remember that we can turn to available resources if the practice of meditation becomes intense. Along with these internal resources, at times when things feel too difficult or intense, it can be a real gift to ourselves to step away from the practice and walk in nature, take a warm bath, get a massage, or spend time with a friend or loved one. As we'll see, kindness and compassion toward ourselves is a foundation of the practice.

It is helpful to think of cultivating a meditation practice as more of an art than a science. Discern what most helps you to be present. What practices and teachers most resonate with you? What qualities (for example, patience, diligence, or kindness) will it serve you to cultivate? What is the quality of the effort you are making—too much striving or too lax?

One of most inspiring reminders I've found in thirty years of meditation is that I can always begin again. No matter how long I may have been caught up in forgetting or lost in daydreams or swept up in an emotion or life situation, I can always come back to this breath, this feeling, this moment.

Ten-Day Mindfulness Meditation for Habit Change

This is a ten-day series of practices that can help you build formal meditation into your life as a bedrock habit. In the upcoming chapters we will integrate the formal practice with the development of skills to create habits that cultivate happiness and well-being.

In this ten-day introduction, we practice sitting for fifteen minutes each day to cultivate present-moment, nonjudging awareness of our experience. We return to our home base, or focus of attention—the breath, the body, or sounds around us—when the mind wanders in order to bring attention to and work with different habit energies that can lead us to unhealthy habitual behaviors.

What follows is a basic outline of the process. However, I highly encourage you to access the full program, which includes detailed and specific steps for each day, available for free online. You have the option of reading written instructions or listening to guided audio; both are available at http://newharbinger.com/44086.

Day 1: Taking your seat and cultivating deep breathing, relaxing the body, and consciously inviting a smile to help the body and mind arrive and settle.

Day 2: Opening to your experience as it is, welcoming the "guests," and saying yes to your present-moment event. Cultivating a kind, accepting, and nonjudging attitude to all that is arising in body, heart, and mind.

Day 3: Grounding your attention by focusing awareness on the breath or other anchor of attention (such as bodily feelings or sounds), and returning to your anchor, or home base, when the mind moves into thought.

Day 4: Meditation on attitude by focusing on the breath, bodily sensations, or sounds. When the mind wanders, returning gently and kindly to your anchor or focus.

Day 5: Three key mindfulness meditation questions that ask, *What am I aware of right now? How am I meeting this experience? What is a wise and kind response?*

Day 6: Meditation on wanting or craving as it arises in the mind and experiencing the feelings without acting on them—simply letting the feelings come and go.

Day 7: Meditation on aversion and resistance as they arise in meditation. Practicing riding the waves of these difficult feelings without acting on them.

Day 8: Meditation on distraction—the things that typically move us toward checking out—and allowing ourselves to experience the feelings without moving away, simply letting them come and go.

Day 9: **Meditation for stress and worry** as these states arise, experiencing the bodily sensations, emotions, and thoughts that accompany them without identifying with or acting on them.

Day 10: **Cultivating self-compassion** and loving-kindness as supportive qualities in abandoning unhealthy habits and developing more beneficial ones.

Cultivating Meditation and Mindfulness Habits

Habit change is not easy, and there will certainly be times when you get off course. However, if you start with a solid foundation, you can minimize your chances of derailment. Here are some tips for making meditation and mindfulness daily bedrock habits:

- Practice the Ten-Day Mindfulness Meditation for Habit Change. (The full guide, along with a series of audio-guided meditations, is available at http://newharbinger.com/44086.)

- At the end of the ten-day period, continue to meditate daily for at least ten to fifteen minutes in silence or by using a guided meditation.

- Experiment with the informal mindfulness practices from earlier in this chapter; find one or two to work with on a daily basis.

- Remember, you can always begin again—this breath, this moment.

Establishing a regular meditation practice and developing the capacity to bring mindfulness to all areas of our life are powerful tools to help us live a more conscious, intentional, and examined life that is aligned with our deepest values and aspirations. In the chapters that follow we integrate these practices with specific skills to support beneficial habit change.

CHAPTER 4

Letting Go of Craving, Cultivating Gratitude

What a bhikkhu [monk or practitioner] *frequently thinks about and ponders on, this becomes the inclination of their mind.*

—Buddha

In the opening chapter we discussed how a key to changing unhealthy habits is to replace them with habits that provide us with a reward, one of a more beneficial kind. That could mean replacing snacking on cookies or cake with eating fruit or nuts. Or it might be replacing angry thoughts with thoughts of kindness and compassion. With practice, over time, we can create new neural pathways and allow the old ones to fade into disuse, thanks to *neuroplasticity*.

We also discussed how our attention is a form of psychic energy and how we can, through practice, choose where we invest our energy for the greatest benefits. In this and later chapters, we'll explore how we can *change the channel* of our attention. We will learn to move our focus from thoughts that lead to rumination, dissatisfaction, or other forms of suffering to habits that are more expansive and conducive to happiness and well-being.

William James spoke of cultivating attention as an "education par excellence" (James 1890)—and when we shift our attention from thinking that doesn't serve us to reflecting in more beneficial ways, we are educating our attention in support of our well-being. Some examples that we will explore include:

- If you are meditating, or even just going about your daily life, and you notice that you are churning out worried thoughts about work, family, or health—the kinds of thoughts that drive you to behave in ways you later regret—you can allow yourself to feel all that you are experiencing (bodily sensations, emotions, and thoughts) and then choose to reflect on things in your life that you are happy about or grateful for.

- If you are judging or criticizing yourself, you can shift to thoughts of kindness and compassion toward yourself, perhaps putting your hand on your heart and sending yourself a wish of happiness: *May I be happy… May I live with ease.*

- If you are craving something that you think will provide you temporary comfort but will likely not be helpful in the long run, you can change the channel to acceptance and gratitude for all that you have.

The nature of craving, aversion, and confusion is to leave us feeling separate and alone. Our vision narrows so that almost all our energy and attention goes to getting what we want or getting away from what we don't like or want—think of an addict's focus on getting their drug. We lose connection with the bigger picture—what we have and what's going well—and until we are able to connect with the larger reality we will stay in the groove of tunnel vision, caught up in suffering.

Changing the channel helps us reconnect with the truth and cultivate emotions and mind states that condition our future states of mind and serve our well-being.

In this and the following three chapters we explore ways of working with habitual thought patterns that lead to experiences or outcomes that are not helpful or do not lead to our well-being. We discuss the four main kinds of *habit energies*, or core impulses or motivations, that lead us toward outcomes that do not serve us: wanting or craving, resistance or aversion, distraction or escaping, and busyness or excessive doing.

There is a wisdom in each of these habit energies. But when we do not respond to our experience with awareness and discernment, they lead to dissatisfaction or suffering. In a nutshell:

- **Wanting or desire** is a natural energy of life that moves us toward getting what we need to survive and thrive. But when met without awareness, this habit energy can result in unhealthy craving, unconscious consumption, addiction, and other forms of suffering.

- The energies underlying **aversion and resistance**—particularly anger and fear—are necessary to keep us safe and defend ourselves against threats to our well-being. But when met without attention, this habit energy can lead to reactive anger, unskillful conflict, harsh self-judgment, and even hatred and war.

- The wish to **disconnect or escape** from what we find boring or uninteresting can help us move toward what enlivens us. But when not met mindfully, this habit energy can lead to disconnection from ourselves, our loved ones, and our priorities, as well as to becoming lost in distraction.

- The energy or impulse toward **busyness and doing** can help us take care of business and be successful and effective. But when met without awareness, this habit energy can lead to anxiety, stress, and workaholism.

We'll explore approaches to working with these habit energies skillfully so that they do not lead to either 1) the difficult mind states and other feelings associated with craving, resistance, busyness, or distraction; or 2) the suffering and dissatisfaction linked to the behaviors that can result from these habit energies (for example, overeating or drinking, smoking, anger, impatience, excessive online engagement, stressful living, procrastination, and so forth).

Working Skillfully with Wanting and Craving

Desire and wanting are fundamental energies of life. Without desire there would be little incentive to do more than the minimum needed to keep ourselves alive. And there would be little reason to travel or explore, investigate how the world works, or engage in new activities or pursuits.

The desire to learn, experience, succeed, flourish, and thrive are natural and potentially beneficial energies that help enhance our lives. When, however, our goals (for example, to feed ourselves, succeed in our work, or have enjoyable experiences) become ends in themselves, or become disconnected from our deeper values and intentions, we experience unpleasantness and suffering. The result could be as basic as a hangover from drinking in excess, persistent craving or neediness from fixating on having something or someone, feeling bloated from eating too much, or a smoker's cough. Or it might be a more existential kind of suffering, such as feeling that we've lost our purpose and meaning in life and that what we are pursuing feels hollow.

It's important to examine our desires and ask ourselves: *Is this a helpful kind of wanting? Does experiencing it lead me to feel tense, tight, contracted, or as if I need to have something to feel okay? Does it lead to an outcome that I don't desire or that causes harm or suffering (such as the excess weight that comes from overeating, or the health consequences of smoking cigarettes)? Or is this a wholesome desire that helps me live with greater ease and freedom?*

Responding to these questions can align us with our deepest intentions that lead to well-being. And from there we can make a commitment to change—to abandon certain behaviors that lead to harm or cultivate others that lead to well-being.

We can then work with the habit energies as they arise in our direct experience—both in meditation and in daily life. Here are ways you can work with these energies and experiences in meditation:

Recognize What You Are Experiencing Without Judgment

When meditating, we can observe the energies that are arising. A first step is to recognize what you are experiencing without judgment, simply being aware of what is arising in the body, the emotions, and the mind.

When you feel the energy of wanting—perhaps manifesting as "I need to have _____" or "I wish I had _____"—bring awareness fully to your experience. What bodily feelings or sensations are you aware of? Perhaps there is a feeling of tension or tightness in the belly; your breathing may be shallow; your muscles might be tense as though you were getting ready to move toward the desired goal or object. Allow yourself to feel these sensations fully. Let them be as big as they want to be. Breathe into the feelings. Make space for them without judgment or resistance, with an attitude of interest and curiosity.

Notice any feelings of moving toward what you are desiring and away from what you are actually feeling, and invite yourself to stay with what is present.

Notice your thoughts—perhaps you are thinking, *This [unpleasant feeling] is going to last forever unless I have* _____. Be aware of the thoughts without believing that they are true; rather, be curious about them. You might even thank the part of your consciousness that is feeling needy for trying to take care of you.

Allow What You Are Experiencing to Come and Go

A second step to observing the energies that are arising is to allow what is present to be here, to come and go in its own time, with kindness and acceptance. Let them come. Let them be. Let them go. Do so without following them or acting on them. With kindness and acceptance let everything come and go without moving toward the habitual behavior or proliferating the habitual patterns of thinking.

When Appropriate, Shift Your Awareness

Move from thoughts of craving and wanting, and reflect on acceptance and gratitude. At times it may be enough to simply be aware of whatever feelings are coming up and allow them to come and go.

The feelings pulling you toward the desired object or experience may dissipate, and you may return to a feeling of ease or calm. But at times the pull toward the desired object may be strong and the thoughts compelling—*I'll feel so much better if I have* _____ or *I'll continue to feel awful if I don't have* _____. This is a situation when it may be helpful to change the channel (see the next topic).

When you notice the thoughts about needing to have the food, drink, drug, or other craving—along with the underlying feelings that may be driving the thoughts—try consciously shifting your awareness to thoughts and reflections of gratitude and acceptance. Since acceptance is a core part of the basic practice of recognizing and allowing, cultivating gratitude is our next focus.

Change the Channel from Craving to Gratitude

When you have practiced wholeheartedly opening to your experience and still feel pulled toward the desired object, try shifting to thoughts of gratitude each time a thought of wanting arises. Think about people, experiences, or situations in your life that you feel grateful for or appreciate: your family and loved ones, dear friends, your health, a financial situation, work, a beautiful day, a comfortable home, your ancestors and all who went before for their efforts that allowed you to be here, life itself, the teachings you've benefited from, your spiritual practice, and so many other gifts that you have received without doing anything particular to earn or deserve them. Allow yourself to reflect on all that you have received and are grateful for, and take in whatever feelings arise.

Make this a consistent practice—when thoughts and feelings of neediness, wanting, or craving arise, consciously choose to reflect on what you are grateful for. Let your consciousness dwell on what you have rather than what you don't have. Let gratitude help open your heart and create neural pathways of appreciation that can grow and expand, while the pathways linked to craving and wanting fall into disuse.

We can support this practice of incorporating gratitude as an antidote to craving with specific *formal* meditations that help make gratitude a core heart quality for us. We can also incorporate thoughts of gratitude into our *informal* everyday practice. Finally, we can also practice gratitude by identifying the habit energy of craving or wanting when it arises in daily life; acknowledging the feelings, emotions, and thoughts that come up; allowing them to come and go; and, when appropriate, choosing to replace them with thoughts of gratitude for all that we have.

Changing the Channel

When we engage in the practice of *changing the channel*—whether toward gratitude, self-compassion, or other quality—it is important to ensure that moving away from the challenging mind state toward the more expansive one is not driven by aversion or resistance. When the motivation is resistance or escape from what we don't like, the shift will likely not be a helpful one—as the expression goes, "What we resist persists." So when we move our attention to avoid a particular feeling, we are not opening to and addressing that feeling—and it will very likely return or persist.

Therefore, it is important to be discerning and ask yourself, *Will it be most helpful to stay with this difficult feeling and open to it, or to move my attention? Am I moving my attention to avoid something, or as a movement toward greater well-being and freedom? What response will serve greater happiness and freedom?*

Don't worry if it's hard to tell between the two at first. As we become more familiar with our habits and patterns of reaction, the strategies and responses that serve us tend to become clearer.

The Power of Gratitude and Its Benefits

Gratitude is a particularly powerful quality to cultivate as an antidote when we are swept up in the energies of wanting, craving, or attachment. When we experience tight, contracted feelings of wanting what we believe will provide happiness, comfort, or release, we lose connection with the fullness of our experience. We undergo a kind of hijacking of our consciousness by one part of our experience. The narrow, survival-based focus of our mind prevents us from being aware of other aspects of our life: our relationships, what's going well, even the beauty of a sunset.

Gratitude has the power to bring us back to our connection with ourselves, with others, and with life itself. When we experience gratitude we cannot at the same time be caught up in craving, anger, or blame. Gratitude neutralizes these states of mind and reconnects us to the web of life.

Extensive scientific research during the past two decades demonstrates a wide variety of benefits from cultivating and practicing gratitude. Robert A. Emmons, a leading researcher and writer on gratitude, summarizes some main benefits:

- Gratitude has one of the strongest links to mental health and satisfaction with life of any personality trait—more than optimism, hope, or compassion.

- Grateful people experience higher levels of emotions such as joy, enthusiasm, love, optimism, and happiness. And gratitude protects us from destructive emotions like envy, resentment, and greed.

- People who experience gratitude can cope better with everyday stress, recover more quickly from illness, and enjoy better physical health.

- People who keep a gratitude journal are 25 percent happier, sleep half an hour more an evening, and exercise 33 percent more each week than those not keeping a journal (Emmons 2013).

- Research has shown that "positive" emotions and mind states such as joy, love, gratitude, and contentment can undo the negative effects of emotions like anger, fear, and shame (Fredrickson 2000).

Gratitude: A Personal Story

As I was beginning to write this book, my mother died. She was ninety-one years old and mother of nine children, with twenty-one grandchildren and eleven great-grandchildren. She was the kindest person I've known, and all my thoughts of her begin and end with gratitude.

Her life took her from New York, where she was born to Irish immigrant parents; to the fishing village in the southwest of Ireland to which they returned when the Great Depression hit and where she spent a happy childhood; to England, where she moved in the mid-1940s and lived the remainder of her life and raised her family.

Her life was far from easy raising nine children on a postal worker's wages in the years after the War, and she struggled to make ends meet. Like so many mothers, her children came first. She carried me up the hill to the hospital when I pulled a pot of boiling treacle on my chest as a toddler; bathed, fed, and clothed us all; and helped us with our homework, even composing poems for my brother and me when our creative juices ran dry.

She loved to walk, and I am grateful to have had the chance to spend many happy days walking with her along small country lanes in Ireland and in the great national parks of the American Southwest, and to remember the simple joy of sitting and reading the newspaper, enjoying the sun in her cottage garden.

I am grateful that she lived long enough that there was nothing that felt left unsaid or unforgiven, no regrets, many joyful moments to remember, and enough opportunity to thank her for a beautiful life, well lived.

I am grateful that in the week after she died I was able to visit her at the funeral home daily, sit with her as she began her onward journey, and thank her for all the love and kindness she had given our family and everyone she came in contact with throughout her life.

The chance to spend time with her after her death was one of the most powerful experiences of my life, for which I'm grateful. It allowed me to feel connected with her spiritually as her post-life journey continued, particularly in the initial weeks after her passing.

I experienced times of connecting with her—in meditation and particularly in the mornings in the state between sleeping and waking. We would be walking together on a path in low foothills. Few words. It was a connection that I could tap into with some ease.

I am grateful that forty-five days after she died I woke up from a dream in which I was with my mother as she moved up and up into the light. It was the most powerful dream I can remember in my life—it felt as real as anything else I've known, with a feeling of ecstasy, of her moving from one realm to another. As I drove home later that day, a big orange full moon hung like a lantern in the sky. Ever since, though the sadness of missing my mother remains, I have had a felt-sense that she is safe, well, and peaceful—and I have no concerns or worries for her.

As I reflect on my mother's life and death, gratitude spontaneously arises. There is so much to be grateful for. And in the weeks after her death, sadness came in waves, but all the grieving was held in an open field of gratitude. The gratitude was large and spacious enough to hold everything that came up—and when I felt stressed or burdened, I chose to shift my thoughts to the gratitude I felt for my mother and, with attention, my mental state would shift and become more spacious.

Gratitude became my main meditation practice, the place that I returned to. And as I inquired into the power of gratitude, I realized that what I was most grateful for was the unconditional love she gave me and all our family. It is the teaching I take from her life—her transmission of unconditional love that I experienced and can share with others.

Gratitude Practice

Is gratitude a practice that you have explored? If it is, you'll know how it can help make a shift from self-absorption—being caught up in the worries, fears, and stickiness of our life—into an experience of greater openness and connection with all of life. If gratitude practice is new to you, I encourage you to explore readings, talks, and meditations on gratitude, beginning with the following simple practices:

- *Reflect on what you are grateful for daily.* Taking time regularly can help you make gratitude a central quality and practice of your life. It can be just a few minutes each day—at the beginning or end of the day, for example—when you focus on and allow yourself to experience deeply your appreciation for the gifts and blessings that enhance your life.

- *Keep a gratitude journal.* At the end of each day, note some things you are grateful for. This has been shown to be one of the best ways to cultivate the life-changing practice of gratitude and realize its benefits.

- *Redirect unwanted habits with gratitude.* Notice self-judgment, anger, or craving, and when it appears, consciously choose to reflect on things, people, or situations in your life that you are grateful for. This can be a powerful way of redirecting habits of thought and action toward more ease and well-being.

Wanting what we don't have is one of the most powerful and challenging habit energies. It can lead us into many unhealthy habits and even addictions. With mindfulness, we can work with the energies of craving when they arise and learn to open to and accept the feelings that are present. When appropriate, we can shift our awareness to a more beneficial mind state. Gratitude is a particularly strong and helpful antidote to craving, as it shifts our focus from what we want and lack to all that we have to be grateful for.

CHAPTER 5

From Judgment and Anger to Kindness

When we experience unpleasantness, pain, or discomfort, or feel threatened, our natural response is to resist, defend ourselves, or escape from the cause of the pain.

There can be wisdom in being critical or remorseful about our own actions or in getting angry with someone who is causing harm. But it is also common for reactions of judgment, anger, or resistance to be a cause of suffering—for example, when we internalize critical self-judgments and continually beat ourselves up or inveterately blame or criticize others.

I once worked with a woman, Lisa, who had recently left an abusive marriage. She shared with me how she had internalized voices of self-criticism and blame over many years and came to believe that these stories were "the truth." She'd been in intense fear and anxiety toward the end of her marriage, thanks to her partner's name-calling, criticism, simmering anger, and explosive rage. Lisa would justify his behavior and blame herself for the abuse, thinking that she needed to be better so that she could save him.

The trauma lasted even after Lisa finally left. She trusted very few people, and the criticisms he leveled at her continued to play over and over in her mind, producing feelings of worthlessness, sadness, resentment, anger, and regret that she couldn't get rid of.

It wasn't until Lisa began learning and recognizing that she had a choice in how she responded to painful thoughts—and that she could respond with compassion and kindness—that she began to really recover.

"Gradually," she said, "I stopped believing the lies, the doubt, and the fear that held me in this cramped, closed-up little space. I learned to feel my feelings rather than shut them down, bottle them up, or try to escape them. I brought awareness to the spiraling, ruminative stories I had internalized over the years from the abuse and saw that they were stories—they were not the truth. Releasing the regrets and forgiving myself gave closure to my suffering. I came to see that there was so much more than the stories I'd come to believe—there is abundance, joy, peace. I never in my wildest dreams believed I'd feel peace and joy again, but now these feelings are available to me."

Lisa stressed to me and now shares with her own students that the process of finding her way out of what she calls "my dark prison" was not a simple or easy journey, but, for her, mindfulness and deepening compassion for herself provided the key to a new life.

Working Skillfully with Resistance and Aversion

Resisting pain, difficulty, and suffering is wired into us by evolution. As we've discussed, this self-protective impulse can truly be a survival mechanism in conditions of threat (for example, running toward higher ground on hearing news of a possible tsunami). But when these self-protective responses linked to fear, anger, and other forms of resistance are reified, solidified, or identified with in the absence of awareness—as Lisa did as a way of protecting herself—they become a source of suffering. Bringing our conditioned responses into awareness can be the difference between perpetuating unhealthy habits and moving toward greater well-being.

We will explore in this chapter the two main directions taken by aversion and resistance:

- Toward oneself, as expressed in self-judgment, self-hatred, the "inner critic," and other forms of self-criticism

- Toward others or the world, manifesting in anger, hostility, frustration, and other expressions of aversion

We'll also discuss and practice how to change the channel to kindness and compassion, where helpful and appropriate.

Meeting Judgment and Self-Criticism

Many of us take setbacks, disappointments, and losses out on ourselves. We judge ourselves harshly: *I'm such a failure, I just can't get things together, Nothing seems to go right for me, I don't have any discipline/willpower/_____.*

These beliefs and inner messages to ourselves often go way back in our lives. We may have received messages from our parents or caregivers like, "You won't be loved unless you act in a certain way/succeed at school/_____." Or we may have drawn conclusions that we need to meet certain standards or benchmarks in order to be loved, to be safe, or to succeed in life.

These messages and beliefs can be pervasive and intensive, as in Lisa's case. We become our own taskmaster, internalizing voices of criticism and judgment. And when we fall short in our behavior or fail in some way, we may respond more harshly to ourselves than we ever would to a friend or family member in similar circumstances.

These beliefs and judgments about ourselves can create real suffering in our lives, constraining us and keeping us on the treadmill of perfectionism and control. We can come to see these voices as part of the "way we are" when in fact they are conditioned patterns—unhelpful and painful habits of thought that have developed through repetition over time. And just as they've developed and seemed to become part of who we are, they can be abandoned through repetition over time.

The process of transforming entrenched habits involves five steps:

1. Deepening *awareness* of the habit pattern

2. Establishing a strong *intention* to change

3. *Recognizing the trigger* to respond in the habitual way

4. *Allowing* our experience to come and go—meeting it with kindness, acceptance, and curiosity

5. *Changing the channel* to self-compassion, where appropriate

1. Deepen Awareness of the Self-Judgment Habit

The more familiar you are with your habits of self-judgment and criticism, the more you are able to see the price you pay for these habits—how they prevent you from living to your full potential—and the more you are able to make beneficial choices.

So take some time to explore how you respond with criticism or self-judgment to setbacks, difficulties, and other challenging situations. Without trying to change anything, simply notice, with compassionate curiosity:

Do voices of judgment and criticism come up incessantly, occasionally, or only in particular circumstances or in relation to specific people or areas of life?

When do they typically arise?

Do particular mind states (tiredness, hunger, loneliness, or worry, for example) trigger or accompany the voices of critical self-judgment?

What do you sense the goal of these voices to be—to take care of you, prevent you from making mistakes, or some other objective?

Is there a kernel of truth or valuable information in the judgments?

And how do these judgments affect your mood or sense of well-being?

Give yourself time to become familiar with these expressions of aversion or resistance that are directed inward toward yourself. See them as conditioned habits of thought that may have played a self-protective role. Ask yourself, *Are these beliefs and judgments helpful to me in my life? Or are they keeping me locked in suffering?*

Don't move too quickly to change them. Rather, begin by getting to know the voices well and meeting them with kindness.

2. Establish the Intention to Make Change

If your critical and judgmental thinking is not serving your well-being, reflect on your commitment to change this habit of judging. How important is it to you to make a change? Are you willing to make the effort to bring awareness to the habit when it arises and stay with uncomfortable feelings that come up in order to develop new, healthier patterns?

If, on reflection, it is important and worth the effort, make a commitment. You might say to yourself, *I will be attentive to inner voices of judgment and harsh criticism. And when they appear, I will recognize them and meet them with kindness. And, when appropriate, I will replace these negative messages with an intention and wish of compassion or loving-kindness toward myself.*

3. Recognize the Inner Critic as a Trigger

Pay attention in daily life and in formal meditation to the inner voices of criticism and judgment. This awareness is key to undermining the power of entrenched habits. They flourish, as we have seen, in the garden of unconsciousness. And when we see them, they cease to have such a strong hold on us.

There is a world of difference between being criticized by your boss and then, on one hand, judging yourself as a failure and believing your self-critical thoughts and, on the other, noticing this harsh voice of self-judgment and seeing it simply as a thought—not *the truth*—and meeting it with kindness.

There are stories in the Buddhist tradition of Mara, a tempter figure, who is an archetype of the forces of greed, hatred, and delusion. It was Mara who appeared when Siddhartha (the Buddha-to-be) sat under the tree on the night of his awakening. Mara offered sensual delights to tempt Siddhartha from his search and questioned the Buddha's authority to claim he was enlightened. As a testament to his awakening, the Buddha touched the ground and said, "The earth is my witness."

Mara also appeared after the Buddha's awakening, but each time he did, the Buddha would say, "I see you, Mara," and Mara would scurry away. Like Mara, when our entrenched habits are seen, their power is weakened because habits perpetuate themselves in unconsciousness. So recognizing judgment and self-criticism when they arise is key to making change.

You might bow (metaphorically) to this habit pattern, recognize that it is motivated by a wish to take care of yourself and keep you safe, and then meet it with kindness and compassionate curiosity.

4. Meet Experiences with Kindness and Acceptance

Bring a kind and accepting awareness to all aspects of what appears when the inner voice of judgment arises. Meet your arising bodily sensations with kindness. Let them come and go. Allow emotions that arise to come and go—there might be sadness or anger at the situation, or grief at the suffering these voices have caused you over the years. You might put your hand on your heart and wish yourself well. Let the feelings come. Let them be. Let them go. Hear the voices as they manifest as thoughts and beliefs, and let them come and go without believing them or identifying with them. Treat them as simply thoughts coming and going, like clouds passing through an open sky.

The spiritual teacher Eckhart Tolle has said, "What we allow we go beyond." When we can let ourselves experience difficult sensations, painful emotions, or challenging thoughts and memories, their hold over us begins to fade, allowing us to experience greater freedom and ease in our lives.

5. Change the Channel to Self-Compassion

Just as we can bring our attention back to the breath when we become aware that our mind has drifted into discursive thought in meditation, so too can we choose to replace a negative or judgmental thought with an intention and wish of kindness and compassion toward ourselves.

Self-compassion means meeting ourselves and our experience with kindness and friendliness. It means accepting ourselves as we are, being kind, and wishing ourselves well. It is an ideal antidote to the harsh and judgmental voice of our inner critic.

So when the habitual voice of judgment appears, recognize it, bow to it, and meet it with kindness. Then choose consciously to replace the thought with a wish of compassion to yourself. You might simply place your hand on your heart and say, *May I be happy…, May I be safe…, May I be kind to myself…, I care about this suffering,* or whatever words, feelings, or images best send a message of compassion toward yourself.

In the coming days, try working with this practice of meeting inner voices of judgment and self-criticism with kindness—both when they arise in formal meditation practice and when they come up in daily life. We will typically have more time and space to work with these voices when they arise in meditation. And giving time and attention to working with the inner critic in a formal practice can be transformative in changing deeply ingrained habits and beliefs about ourselves, our abilities, our goodness, and so much else.

You may not have the same opportunity to work in depth with voices of self-judgment in daily life (for example, when you've said or done something you feel embarrassed about). In these situations, what may be most possible is a kind of "mindfulness first aid"—opening to whatever feelings and emotions are present and sending yourself a wish of compassion or loving-kindness. Then coming back later and exploring what, if anything, you might have done differently or what you can learn from the experience.

Habits of Resistance to Others and the World

When we experience something that feels unpleasant (a loud noise, an angry gesture toward us, or a feeling of bodily pain or discomfort, for example), we respond by resisting or moving away from the unpleasant feeling to bring ourselves back to a state of equilibrium or comfort. Our brain and nervous system are programmed by evolution to respond to perceived threats to our safety by fighting, fleeing, or freezing. As we've discussed, this is a natural protective response that has helped us survive and thrive.

But these responses of resisting or pushing away what is unpleasant or threatening can become habitual in situations that do not serve our well-being. Examples include when appropriate concern about the future turns into anxiety and stress through repetitive thinking, when reflection on a past event becomes ruminating over and over on what happened, and when anger about what someone said turns into hatred of the person through repeatedly telling ourselves what a terrible person they are. In these situations, lack of awareness and repeated acting out of a response can turn almost any situation involving unpleasant feelings into an unhealthy habit that impacts our lives.

We all have our unique expressions of responding in unwise or unhelpful ways to feelings of unpleasantness:

Do you find yourself habitually getting angry with your children or other family members in particular situations, such as when getting kids ready for school, talking about finances, or discussing politics?

Do you habitually judge others for the choices they've made or how they look?

Do you get triggered by listening to people you disagree with when watching TV?

Do you feel impatient when other drivers are not going fast enough for you?

Do you notice yourself being habitually annoyed, impatient, frustrated, or angry at how the world is, how others behave, or how things are not going as you want them to?

In any situation where unpleasantness comes up, we can change what is possible to change, and then we have two choices: to *accept* what can't be changed—this is the path of mindfulness, bringing a kind, nonjudging awareness to this experience as it is—or to *resist* what we don't like, struggle with it, tell ourselves and others how it should be different, and suffer as a consequence of resisting life as it is unfolding.

In the same way as we worked with aversion that turns inward—in the form of self-judgment and self-criticism—we can bring the tools of mindful awareness to work wisely with aversion when it is directed outward toward others and the world. We can use the same five-step habit-transformation approach with some adaptations.

1. Deepen Awareness of Aversion and Resistance Habits

As you go about your day, pay attention to when you habitually get caught in habits of aversion that manifest as anger, impatience, frustration, annoyance, jealousy, blame, sadness, judgment, regret, and other habitual responses of wanting situations or people to be different than they are.

When do these patterns of aversive responses come up? Is there a particular time they appear (for example, when driving to work you get impatient)?

Where do these feelings and responses typically come up (for example, at work feeling envious or isolated around colleagues)?

Who is involved? Is this habit triggered by, or by being with, a particular person or people? Perhaps it is a reaction of anger or defensiveness that only or mostly comes up in discussions with a partner.

What feels unpleasant or difficult about this situation? It might be a feeling of sadness that arises as you recognize that a habit of judgment or defensiveness is creating separation from a loved one.

How do you feel when you are caught up in this habitual response? What do you notice in your body, emotions, and mind? Tension? Tightness? Racing thoughts? Feeling stuck?

A key step in changing habits is to become aware of the habit you created and see clearly the ways in which it is not helping you. The more you can deepen this awareness, the more you can bring the pattern into the light so that you can choose to make a change. Awareness is the foundation for making change. So the emphasis is first on becoming familiar with the pattern, the context, and all the elements that help trigger the habit and make it automatic and unconscious.

2. Establish an Intention to Make Change

As in working with self-judgment and criticism, ask yourself how important it is to bring change to this area of your life. Are you prepared to do the necessary work of paying attention? Are you willing to open to the difficult feelings, emotions, and mind states associated with this habit of resistance—without acting out the habit?

If the answer is yes, make a commitment to yourself to meet this unhealthy habit with compassionate awareness when it arises in your life. And stay connected with your intentions as you work to change this habit.

3. Recognize the Habit of Aversion and Resistance

You've taken time in step 1 to become familiar with the habit—when, where, how, and why it arises—and the price you are paying for it in your life. In this third step you actively engage with the habit and how it manifests.

When familiar feelings (such as annoyance, impatience, or judgment of another person, or frustration with a situation) arise, recognize this habit of mind that you are seeking to change and commit to meet it with kindness and acceptance—say, "I see you, Mara." Recognizing your experience is a key to making change.

4. Let the Feeling of Resistance Come and Go

When you feel triggered by what someone is doing, or by something that isn't going "right" (such as being stuck in traffic or having a difficult conversation with a company representative on the phone), you have two main choices: One is to habitually act out your feelings, even if this leads to suffering for yourself or others. The other is to choose to stay with the difficult sensations, emotions, and thoughts with awareness, recognizing what you are experiencing and allowing the feelings and thoughts to come and go.

The more you build the muscle of "recognizing and allowing," the more you bring into play choices of how to respond. As the Tibetan Buddhist teacher Mingyur Rinpoche said, "Ultimately, happiness comes down to choosing between the discomfort of becoming aware of your mental afflictions and the discomfort of being ruled by them" (Mingyur 2007).

5. Change the Channel

An ideal antidote for working with anger, frustration, blame, and other forms of aversion or resistance is to consciously invite the quality of loving-kindness to arise in the mind. Often it isn't easy because the story in our mind about "how wrong this person is" or "how mean they are" is strongly active in our reptilian, fight-or-flight brain. With training and practice, we can strengthen our capacity to remember the possibility of shifting from *identification* with what we are believing into *kind awareness* of our experience.

When you are able to remember, you can then consciously choose to wish well to the other person—perhaps remembering that anyone who is causing suffering is themselves suffering, that all of us wish to be happy. You can begin by recognizing that when you are caught up in anger, judgment, or blame, you are suffering.

You can send wishes of kindness and compassion to yourself, and then go outward to include others: *May I be happy... safe... free from suffering. May you too be happy... safe... free from suffering...*

Practice: Shifting from Aversion to Compassion

In the coming days, take time to notice when resistance or aversion arise in one of their many forms: anger, frustration, impatience, judgment, blame, and so on. Then choose to shift from identification with the story into awareness, taking the five steps:

1. Awareness

2. Intention

3. Recognizing

4. Allowing

5. Changing the channel

Or even just one step can be appropriate. Notice what it feels like in the body, emotions, and mind to shift out of aversion into kindness and compassion.

The habit energies of judgment, anger, and other expressions of aversion are powerful ones, primed in us by millions of years of evolution. But they do not need to be a source of suffering. When seen and met with acceptance they can come and go and, when appropriate, can be replaced by loving-kindness or compassion.

CHAPTER 6

Distraction and the Power of Awareness

When I came to meditation in my thirties, I had a sense of coming home. It took me back to two kinds of experiences from childhood: One was the feeling of peace I had at the age of nine or ten, when I'd go and sit in a big neighborhood tree and be alone for a couple of hours—nothing to do, no agenda, just a sense of peace and well-being.

The other was playing football (a.k.a. soccer) in my mid- and late-teens and experiencing a pure kind of joy. Our school team was successful. We'd played together for many years and knew each other's style of play well. But it's not the victories or trophies I remember most but the feeling of joy I now recognize as "flow"—a falling away of self-consciousness and the experience of being fully present in running and moving, passing, tackling, and shooting without being caught up in the future or any agenda other than exactly what I was doing in that moment.

These experiences of peace and the joy of being fully present contrasted with other times: when I felt preoccupied with the future and how I was doing in school, and when occasional lack of focus and direction would draw me to whatever seemed to be calling in that moment. I didn't realize then that these polarities—peace and agitation, being joyfully present and being distracted or disconnected—are hardwired into our brain through millions of years of evolution.

When we are not focused and paying attention, we are typically lost in thought, AWOL from ourselves and our experience, and it's mainly not fun. In this chapter, we'll explore the habits of distraction that can often lead us to get lost in thought or to become agitated—and the way we can cultivate attention to address these habits at their root.

Being Here or Being Lost— the Neuroscience

The nature of our mind when we are not specifically paying attention (for example, focusing on what we are doing, concentrating on a task, or meditating) is to wander. This appears, in computer language, to be a feature, not a bug. Rather than being an evolutionary glitch, mind-wandering seems to have provided a survival advantage, and it continues to offer some benefits today. But like so much else involving our brain, there is also a significant downside.

Neuroscience studies in recent years point to two main modes of *self-awareness*, which is the way the brain functions depending on how we are paying attention and what we are focusing on. When you are in a resting state, you typically default to a *narrative focus*, whereby you are thinking of the past or future, or comparing yourself to others; this mode of awareness is associated more with negative than positive feelings. When you are in an *experiencing focus*, specifically bringing awareness to your experience and paying attention to what's happening here and now, there is less rumination and mind-wandering; this mode is associated more with positive feelings.

There were likely evolutionary survival benefits in the narrative or mind-wandering mode—providing our ancestors the opportunity to process information and develop new solutions to problems. And many great insights and inventions have come in these resting states. Most of us can probably recall creative insights, understandings, or breakthroughs that have come when we put aside deliberate attempts to solve a problem or think something through. For myself, when writing *The Here-and-Now Habit*, three or four of my main insights came when I was not focused on writing but relaxing and walking in the woods after a period of focused attention.

But while clear benefits come from the narrative or default mode, much of the thinking we do in this non-focused mode is associated with more ruminative, anxious, stressed, and distracted thinking, which we typically experience as unpleasant.

A study by Matthew Killingsworth and Daniel Gilbert (2010) of Harvard University asked 2,250 adults questions about what they were doing when contacted via a phone app, whether they were thinking about what they were doing or something else, and whether their experience was pleasant or unpleasant. The researchers found that: respondents' minds wandered frequently (46.9 percent of the time); they were less happy when their mind was wandering than when it wasn't; and what they were thinking was a better predictor of their happiness than what they were doing.

Killingsworth and Gilbert concluded, "[A] human mind is a wandering mind, and a wandering mind is an unhappy mind. The ability to think about what is not happening is a cognitive achievement that comes at an emotional cost" (2010, 932).

It seems clear from studies of where our minds go when we are not paying attention that we pay a high price for the creative insights that occasionally fall in our laps—and that we can train our minds to make being present here and now our default mode. Significantly, studies have found that meditators are better able to access the experiencing mode and uncouple from the narrative mode than nonmeditators (Farb et al. 2007; Killingsworth and Gilbert 2010).

So we have a choice: to consciously cultivate attention through mindfulness and related practices, and experience the benefits, or allow our attention to go to what is calling most strongly for attention. In an age when the evidence of increased distraction is everywhere and the human costs are immense—3,477 people were killed in 2015 in the United States by distracted driving (NCSA 2017)—the benefits of cultivating attention are clear. And practices are available to support developing a calm, focused mind. We will explore some of these practices in the next section.

Working Skillfully with Distraction

The skills and practices presented in chapter 3 for cultivating a meditation practice and developing mindfulness skills in daily life are a powerful support in building the muscle of attention and working with habits of distraction. We will use and build on those skills in this chapter and in chapter 9, as we explore the particular challenges of distraction and the behaviors that spring from or reflect a distracted mind: multitasking, being on autopilot, daydreaming, spending large swaths of time online, and more.

Our happiness and freedom depend on whether we train our mind. The Buddha said that nothing can do you more harm than an untrained mind, and nothing and no one can do you more good than a trained mind (Nyanaponika Thera and Bodhi 1999) An untrained mind will gravitate toward unconscious and unexamined habits, as well as toward behaviors that cause ourselves and others harm. With a trained mind, we strengthen our capacity to choose words, actions, and thoughts that support well-being and happiness for ourselves and others.

Here are two practices to help you notice when you are caught up in distraction and how to come back to the present moment. You're also invited to explore formal practices to deepen the power of concentration, which helps incline the mind toward steadiness and presence.

As you explore these practices, keep in mind that you can't untangle yourself from unhealthy habits unless you are aware that you are acting them out. In order to be able to choose how you respond in any given moment to what you are experiencing, you first need to remember to pay attention—to check in with yourself: *Where is my attention now? What am I experiencing?*

If you have not trained yourself to come back to this moment, your attention inevitably goes to what is most compelling, shiny, tasty, or annoying—or to where in similar conditions the mind has habitually gone in the past.

Cultivating the Art of Remembering

This practice is for cultivating attention and stepping out of distraction many times throughout the day for short periods.

We can't make ourselves remember. Remembering, like thinking, happens. But we can strengthen our likelihood of remembering by repeatedly bringing our attention back to our present-moment experience. Ironically, the same technology that can play a big role in distraction can also help us train our minds to come home to the here and now.

You can adapt this practice, which involves using a timer, to your own needs and schedule. The advantage of using an alarm is that it outsources the responsibility of remembering to a device—you don't have to remember to remember—and with practice you can internalize and strengthen your capacity to remember. (The app Mindfulness Bell functions well.)

1. Set an alarm on your phone or computer to ring at regular intervals (say, every fifteen or twenty minutes) or sporadically (three or four times an hour, for example).

2. When the bell rings (or vibrates), stop whatever you are doing, if possible.

3. If you are in a meeting, conversation, or other activity that prevents you from taking a minute or two to pause, you might simply deepen your breathing and bring attention to how you are feeling and where your attention is when the bell rings. The bell is your reminder to re-arrive in this

moment and to be aware of and engaged with whatever you are doing at that time.

4. If you have the opportunity for a longer and fully attentive pause (say, you are working at home, walking, or resting), pause what you are doing when the bell rings and bring attention fully to your experience. Notice how your body feels: tense, relaxed, neutral... Bring awareness to any mood or emotional state: sadness, excitement, numbness...

   Ask yourself, *Where was my attention when the bell rang? Was I present or was my mind elsewhere?* If your mind was caught up in thinking, notice the kind of thinking: planning, judging, comparing, worrying, ruminating, problem solving, daydreaming... Ask yourself, *Was it pleasant, unpleasant, or neutral to be engaged in this kind of thinking?*

   Notice whether this is a kind of thinking that you spend a lot of time caught up in (worrying about the future, for example, or ruminating, or judging yourself for something you did or didn't do). Ask yourself, *Does this thinking lead toward greater happiness and freedom? Or does it leave me feeling tight, contracted, limited, or stuck in narrow thoughts or beliefs—and consequently suffering?*

5. It may be clear that the thinking you were engaged in wasn't helpful and that it will serve you well to notice whenever you are caught up in this kind of thinking, so

that you can come back to your direct experience. But, first, it's helpful to ask, *Is there something that is useful in this thinking—a nugget of wisdom or a way in which a part of myself is trying to keep me safe or happy?*

You may be worrying about a presentation you have to give in a week that you are behind in preparing for. You might see that the worrying is only making you more stressed and tense, but, nevertheless, this situation is calling for your attention.

6. Write down any useful steps you can take (such as planning for the presentation) or commitments you want to make (such as setting aside time each day to work on a project). Then let them go for now.

7. When you have noticed where your attention was when the timer sounded—and what you were thinking about and whether it was helpful thinking—let your attention come back to your experience here and now. Feel your breathing, bring awareness to your bodily sensations, open to whatever emotions or mind states are present, experiencing the environment you are in and what is going on around you. Notice any difference between how it feels to be here now compared with how it felt when you became aware you were lost in thought. Is there any noticeable difference between the direct experience in this moment and being lost in the virtual reality of mind wandering? See if you can drop into this moment—just this... nothing missing... nowhere else to go or be...

Let the sound of the bell be a reminder to be here and come out of thoughts. With training and repetition, our practice of coming back comes more naturally—and ultimately more automatically, in the way putting a seatbelt on when we get in a car becomes automatic. We can look at these moments of coming home to our direct experience as like the dots of a pointillist painting—as the dots become more pervasive, this state becomes the prevailing or default quality of the mind, just as the dots make up and fill out the main images in the painting.

Each time we come back to our senses, to our direct experience, we have a glimpse of the aliveness and freedom that are our natural state—and we can recognize that our typical, everyday mode of ruminating, worrying, and spacing out are simply ways in which we forget and disconnect from our aliveness.

Another way we connect to our aliveness is through meditation. The main focus of the meditations we've been exploring in this book is mindfulness—a quality of present-moment, nonjudging awareness of our experience. Focusing our attention (for example, by using an object, such as the breath) is an important part of mindfulness practice, but concentration is not the main goal or objective of mindfulness meditation. Rather, the intention is to cultivate a receptive, openhearted awareness that allows us to meet all of our experience—the joys and sorrows, pains and pleasures—with acceptance and kindness.

Meditation to deepen *concentration*, however, can be of great benefit for stabilizing and focusing the mind, so that we are less inclined to be swept up in distractions. It also allows for cultivating deeper states of focus and absorption. Where mindfulness is a broad, inclusive awareness that is conscious of what is present, like a wide-angle lens on a camera, concentration is one-pointed, focusing on a particular object, like a zoom lens on a camera.

Formal Concentration to Focus the Mind

Strengthening your capacity for one-pointed awareness can be a powerful support in cultivating a nondistracted mind. Here is a simple concentration meditation practice to try.

1. Begin by finding a comfortable, relaxed posture—on a chair, cushion, or bench. Sit with your back straight, shoulders relaxed, your chest open to receive the breath, and eyes closed or open, with a soft, unfocused gaze. Invite a smile or half smile to help relax the brain and nervous system.

2. Take a few long, deep breaths to help relax the body and mind. Consciously put aside plans and memories, and commit to being as fully present as you can be for the period of meditation.

3. Choose an object on which to focus attention. There are many possibilities. One of the most commonly used and helpful—because it is always available to us—is your own breathing. We'll use the breath as the template for practice here.

4. Bring your attention to your breathing just as it is, without deepening or modifying it. You can focus your attention at the place where you are most aware of your breathing or most at ease with it, such as the feeling of the breath at the tip of the nostrils, or the experience of the chest or abdomen rising and falling. Let your own breathing be the focus of your attention, with a friendly and curious awareness.

5. Follow the sensations of breathing through the inhalation, the exhalation, and the pause, and the next inhale, exhale, and pause... If it helps stabilize your attention, you can mentally note *in* for the in-breath and *out* for the out-breath, or *rise* for the rising of the chest or abdomen, and *fall* for the falling.

6. When your attention moves into thought, gently and diligently bring it back to the experience of breathing. If a strong emotion arises, simply notice it and bring your attention back to your breathing. Anytime you become aware of other experiences, bring your attention back to the breath.

7. Continue practicing in this way through to the end of your period of meditation, directing attention to the breath and returning when you become aware that attention has drifted.

When we regularly schedule these practices, we cultivate the capacity to let go of distractions and be present for our experience. We also develop a mind that is more stable, focused, and present. And we deepen our experience of peaceful and calm awareness. Over time, with practice, the quality of presence—being truly present here and now for our experience—becomes the default mode of our mind rather than being lost in plans, stories, worries, and daydreams.

CHAPTER 7

Working Mindfully with Stress and Busyness

It's not the stress but how you handle it which dictates its effects on the mind and the body.

—Jon Kabat-Zinn

Stress and the way we respond to stressful situations and experiences is a major factor in the formation of habits and in changing habits. When we are able to respond effectively to stress, we can typically recover and return to a balanced response to life—without the painful effects of being stressed out or indulging in harmful behaviors.

When we respond to stress unconsciously or in other unhelpful ways, we can easily get caught up in the unpleasant feelings of stress reactivity. This can lead us to get swept up in busyness and excessive doing as we seek to solve the problem of stress "out there" rather than by opening to what we are experiencing here and now, and letting the feelings come and go.

It's also common to take refuge in the unhealthy habits that we'll discuss in the chapters that follow (smoking, eating or drinking unwisely, getting angry, procrastinating, escaping into devices, and so forth). Being stressed out, anxious, overwhelmed, constantly busy, or always on our way somewhere are themselves typically unhealthy habitual behaviors that come from meeting perceived threats or challenges in unhelpful or unconscious ways.

In this chapter, we'll discuss the relationship of stress to our habits—and how we can respond mindfully and consciously to stress in order to help us avoid or let go of unhealthy habits and cultivate beneficial ones. We'll explore: what stress is and the societal and individual price we pay for stress; the difference between responding wisely and unwisely to stress, as well as the consequences of each approach; and the ways our responses to stress can play a major role in developing and changing habits. We'll also look at how mindfulness can help us work skillfully with stress and support us in cultivating healthy life habits. We'll finish by presenting ways of meeting stress with mindfulness in the moment.

Stress and Its Impact

Stress is an inevitable and natural part of life, but it can be dangerous—even deadly—when it becomes a chronic and habitual way of reacting to life's challenges.

Stress can be understood as any experience during which the demands of a situation exceed an individual's perceived ability to cope. Described in a simplified way: a perception of threat or danger activates the *stress response*—or fight-flight-freeze mode—of the *sympathetic nervous system* (the branch of the nervous system that developed to help mobilize the resources of body and mind to respond to life-threatening situations), triggering the release of chemicals (cortisol and adrenaline). The stress response also triggers an increase in blood pressure, breathing, and heart rate; an increase in blood pumping to the muscles that can respond effectively to the challenge; and the temporary shutdown of unnecessary functions, such as reproduction and digestion. When these mind-body responses are mobilized, we have our foot pressed down on the (metaphorical) gas pedal ready to react optimally to the threat (Mohd 2008).

In a healthy stress response, we are able, once the threat has passed, to relax and come back to balance, or homeostasis. The parasympathetic nervous system, like the brakes on a car, then allows us to "rest and digest" and support healthy recovery from the activation.

However, it's also possible to keep the stress response activated—staying in fight-or-flight mode—after the threat has passed or even when we think about something worrisome in the future. Our thought processes can keep our body activated and ready to respond to the threat, even when, objectively, the situation may not be threatening. Believing that we are under threat is enough—and our perceptions and beliefs keep the release of stress hormones, increased blood pressure, heart rate, and the like going with the potential for harmful physical and mental health outcomes. The unhealthy and unhelpful reaction to a stressful experience is termed *stress reactivity* (Kabat-Zinn 2013), which we will distinguish from a healthy stress response

Moreover, in seeking short-term comfort from the unpleasantness generated by stress, we often make things worse with unhealthy ways of coping, including drugs, alcohol, cigarettes, caffeine, and food. These things can, depending on the substance, compound the stress and place further pressure on the brain and digestive, nervous, immune, and cardiovascular systems. They can also manifest in increased blood pressure, sleep disorders, headaches, insomnia, chronic anxiety, and a variety of other conditions.

The increased pressures, demands, and pace of life—accompanied by ways of responding to and coping with stress that often exacerbate the situation—have led to a stress crisis in the United States:

- An estimated 75 to 90 percent of all visits to primary care physicians are for stress-related complaints (Boone and Anthony 2003).

- 43 percent of all adults suffer adverse health effects from stress (WebMD 2017).

- Stress is linked to all of the leading causes of death: heart disease, cancer, lung ailments, accidents, cirrhosis, and suicide (Boone and Anthony 2003).

- An estimated 1 million workers are absent on an average workday because of stress-related complaints (Boone and Anthony 2003).

- Job-related stress is estimated to cost U.S. industry $300 billion annually (WebMD 2017).

Beyond the statistics, we know how challenging stress can be in our daily lives. The good news is that we have a significant say in how stress affects us—depending on how we respond. Mindfulness can play a major role in lessening stress and supporting greater ease and well-being. This happens through working wisely with stress that arises in meditation; in meeting the stresses of daily life mindfully;

and in developing healthy life habits that can inoculate us against some of the impacts of stress.

Responding vs. Reacting to Stress

Let's look at one stressful scenario with two different outcomes: Martha has a job that she enjoys at a tech company and has been asked to give a presentation that could bring the company a new level of visibility and growth. She feels excited, nervous, and honored to be asked to take on such an important responsibility.

Outcome 1: After her initial feeling of excitement and pride, Martha starts having doubts about her ability. She feels like an imposter and thinks the boss must have made a mistake in choosing her. She thinks about how little time she has to prepare and imagines scenarios where she performs poorly, her firm loses the contract, and she is increasingly sidelined within the company. Martha's fears make it hard to sleep, and she worries that she won't be productive at work. Her worries make it difficult to keep up with the demands at work.

At home Martha is snappy with her family and feels increasingly alone. She eats sweets, smokes a few cigarettes to lessen the anxious feelings, and drinks wine before bed to help her sleep. She wakes after a couple of hours worrying about the presentation and the work that she's behind on.

The cycle gets worse each day as she feels the stress in her body and gets caught up in negative thinking. She wonders how to get out of the cycle: *Maybe I should tell my boss that I can't make the presentation... Or maybe I should seek medication... Or look into therapy...*

Outcome 2: After her initial excitement, Martha begins to feel nervous and anxious: *Can I do this? Maybe they should have asked my colleague, Jamila... What if I mess it up?* She sees how tense she is and knows if she keeps feeding these thoughts they'll become a self-fulfilling prophecy. So Martha takes some deeper breaths, opens to where she feels this nervousness and anxiety in her body, accepts the physical sensations, and invites those parts of her body to soften. She commits to seeing her thoughts just as thoughts, rather than as "the truth," and to practicing letting them go. Martha talks with her best friend about her hopes and fears, and Sydney is excited and encourages her.

Martha thinks about the presentation like a race, with her needing to be in the best mental and physical shape. She reflects on other times she's faced challenges successfully. She continues to meditate daily, goes to the gym and yoga classes, and takes walks in the park to decompress. She spends time with her kids and commits to being fully present with them. The day before the presentation, Martha feels ready and confident. She doesn't know how it will go but reflects that this is just one thing, not the be-all and end-all, and it will be fine however it turns out.

The Habit of Stress Reactivity

When we repeatedly react to a threat or challenge in ways that keep the threat active and in our consciousness, as Martha does in the first outcome, without giving ourselves the opportunity to recover and come back into balance, we get caught in the *habit of stress reactivity*. Our evolutionary-based survival responses are of great importance to us if we need to jump out of the way of an out-of-control bus. But when they become habits, they mobilize to deal with a situation or experience that isn't actually a threat to our survival but is perceived to be by our mind. When we respond in this way, one part of our experience—the perception of fear and the threat of harm to oneself—takes control and co-opts our consciousness.

We become intensely focused on what we need to do to react effectively and deal with the "threat." This can manifest as intense busyness and "doing," whereby our focus is on getting things done as a way to alleviate the stress. It's like we're being chased by a bear (the stress) and we'll be okay if we can just outrun it (get enough done).

Meanwhile, creativity and the ability to look at the big picture, which require space and ease, go offline because our energies are needed to deal with the threat. Deep concern for others becomes less accessible as our resources are directed toward our personal "emergency." Life, for the time we are caught up in stress reactivity, is focused on mobilizing to respond to the threat. And once we become locked into this stress reaction, it can be difficult to find a way back to a balanced and wise way of being in the world. And, as we've noted, when we're dealing with the unpleasant feelings of stress, we often seek comfort in behaviors and substances that make things worse, compounding the stress cycle.

Mindfulness plays a key role in working with stress (the challenge itself) and stress reactivity (our unhealthy reactions to the challenge). We'll explore how mindfulness and other skillful practices help us meet the stresses of life with compassion and wisdom so that we may live with more ease and well-being.

Working Skillfully with Stress

When we meet stressful situations and experiences without awareness, we easily get pulled into a story line. Typically our mental stories are about bad things that could happen, which can lead to getting caught in a cycle of stress reactivity. As Eckhart Tolle said, "You can always cope with the present moment, but you cannot cope with something that is only a mind projection—you cannot cope with the future" (1999, 35).

Mindfulness invites us to keep coming back to *this* moment, *this* experience, *here and now*. Using the practices of mindfulness—in meditation and in daily life situations—can help us work with stress, as evidenced by the experience of two friends, Zak and Mary, who are going through different stressful challenges.

• Zak's Story

Zak is writing a research article that is due in a few weeks and is worried about getting it finished on time and how it will be received. He wants to avoid reacting to stress in an unproductive way, so he opts to meditate.

As Zak sits in meditation, he feels tightness in his stomach as a thought comes up about how much he still has to do and how short the timeline is to get his article finished. He remembers to recognize the thought as a thought. Then he chooses to let it go and not keep revisiting the question of how much time he has.

A little later, after his mind has been wandering for a while, the thought about the deadline comes back accompanied by a feeling of tension and anxiety in his stomach. He starts to wonder, What if I don't make the deadline? Then my article won't get published, and then my reputation will be destroyed, and then I'll lose credibility, and then I could lose my job.

Before long, Zak finds that he's pulled into his swirling thoughts and underlying fears, which leads to more bodily tension, which leads to more fearful thoughts...

For a moment, he recognizes how wrapped around the axle he has become and is able to bring awareness to his overall experience—the thoughts, sensations, and emotions—and he comes back to his breathing. Zak explores the feeling in his stomach more closely and notices that it has softened a little as he gives space and care to it. With kind attention, he stays with the feeling, allowing it all the space it needs, and when it passes he comes back to his breath.

Working Mindfully with Stress in Daily Life

Just as in formal meditation, you can prevent stress reactivity from arising by bringing present-moment awareness to your experience in daily life situations.

When stressful situations come up, remain present with what you are experiencing. Stay aware of your bodily feelings and pay attention to your breathing. And, when you get agitated or stressed, come back to your breath and invite some deeper breaths to bring you back into balance. Finally, invite a smile to your face—this helps you shift into the rest-and-digest mode of the parasympathetic nervous system.

• Mary's Story

Mary has recently received a diagnosis of cancer and is not sure how serious her condition is. Mary recognizes that her situation is a difficult one, with a worrisome diagnosis and two young kids. She tries to live a healthy life and not keep thinking about all the things that might happen. But daily life, including doctor's visits and medical procedures, brings up situations that trigger her fears for the future: *What if this is an aggressive form of cancer? What will become of my kids if I'm not here to take care of them? What else should I be doing to find a cure? These can all be realistic and helpful questions if posed in a balanced and mindful way.* But if not posed and met with awareness, they can easily turn into catastrophizing and lock us into a habitual stress cycle.

As Mary feels herself being pulled into fear and racing thoughts, she remembers to STOP (see next exercise). This mindfulness skill helps her create some distance from her arising panicky feeling: She takes a few deep breaths, which calms her. She then acknowledges her bodily sensations and emotions. Mary notices tightness in her throat, and then lets it go.

She has the thought, *What if I only have six months to live?* and then lets it go. She invites the sensations and thoughts and allows them to pass. After *a few minutes, Mary directs her attention to the sounds around her; she finds it calming and meditative to listen mindfully for a couple of minutes. Then she goes back to her tasks feeling grounded and recharged.*

STOP Stress in Its Tracks

A simple practice of mindful "first aid" that can be helpful in preventing a stressful situation or experience from turning into full-blown stress reactivity is known by the acronym STOP (Stahl and Goldstein 2010).

- *Stop.* Step back from what you are doing or saying and consciously pause, bringing your attention to your experience.

- *Take breaths.* Inhale deeply and exhale. Do this a few times. Let awareness of your breathing invite a relaxing and calming of your body and mind.

- *Observe.* Notice what is happening. Observe your thoughts without believing they are true. Let them come and go. Bring awareness to your emotions and experience how they are expressed in your body. Pay attention to your bodily sensations and let them come and go.

- *Proceed.* Choose a healthy response, such as returning consciously to your daily activities, taking a mindful walk to establish a sense of calm presence, or sitting quietly for a few minutes.

We can use this practice almost any time to find the space between stimulus and response. We can experience the profound difference between a healthy stress response that allows us to come back to a place of calm and ease, and stress reactivity, where we are swept up in habitual fight-or-flight energies.

As you go through the day, use naturally occurring situations as reminders to come back to your body and to this moment, such as when the phone rings… when you shift from one activity, meeting, or call to another… when you stop at a red light when driving… Take a moment to pause and check in with your experience: *How is my breathing— calm and relaxed or tight and short? Am I feeling tense—where in the body? Am I proliferating anxious, stressful thoughts?* If you notice that you are feeling stressed or anxious, consciously relax your body, taking a few deeper breaths.

Connecting with Our Heart

One of the most powerful ways of untangling ourselves when we are caught in the habit of stress reactivity is to connect with the natural caring we have for ourselves, for others, and for life itself. When we are hooked in stress reactivity, we tend to be shut down, and accessing this caring and connection can be difficult. Cultivating practices of gratitude, self-compassion, loving-kindness, joy, and other heart states can help us step out of reactivity and come back into connection with ourselves and with life.

Let's look at two of these heart states and how you can apply them as a helpful stress response.

Gratitude, which we discussed as an antidote to craving in chapter 4, helps us step out of the isolation of emergency mode and widen our lens to recognize and appreciate all that we have been freely given by others and by life itself. Scientific research has shown the power of gratitude in lessening stress and worry (Emmons 2013).

If you are caught up in a stress reaction, bring to mind three things you are grateful for. Allow yourself to take in and feel your own appreciation for what you have been given and, if you can, touch into whatever sensations and feelings are present in the body. Let yourself experience them for twenty to thirty seconds. Notice if it helps you to step out of a narrow story into a more spacious and openhearted awareness. Whatever you experience, have the intention of meeting it with kindness and acceptance.

Self-compassion, which we explored in chapter 5 as an antidote to self-judgment, helps us meet our own experience with kindness rather than with judgment or criticism (for example, that we "should" be doing a better job in dealing with this stress). The research on self-compassion also shows its benefits in lessening stress (Byrne 2016).

If you are caught up in a habit of stress reactivity, try wishing yourself well, sending a message of caring: *May I be happy… safe… free from stress and worry…* Or quietly say to yourself, *I care about this suffering,* and, putting your hand on your heart, allow yourself to take in your care and concern for yourself…

These qualities of gratitude and self-compassion, along with other heart-opening states (including joy, loving-kindness, forgiveness, and equanimity), all help us step out of our mental story into a more spacious and deeper connection with ourselves and with life. As well as being practiced in many traditions to enhance well-being and happiness, these expansive emotions and mind states have the ability to neutralize more afflictive and "negative" emotions (Fredrickson 2000).

Cultivating Healthy Habits

Another powerful support to avoid getting caught in stress reactivity—or work with it if it has arisen—is to cultivate healthy habits in daily life. If we eat unconsciously, sleep poorly, work too much, or engage in other unhealthy habits, like being busy all the time and running from one task to another, we are setting ourselves up for increased stress to arise—and our reactions to the unpleasantness of stress will likely pull us toward unhealthy behaviors that bring more stress.

On the other hand, when we lead a balanced and healthy life, and cultivate the intention to be present for our experience through the different activities of the day, we create the conditions to meet challenges with awareness. We can also recover more rapidly and fully from stressors that arise.

Some of the most important daily life habits to cultivate are:

- *Movement, exercise, and spending time in nature:* Engaging in regular exercise (running, jogging, walking, cycling, swimming, dancing, yoga, qigong, tai chi, or other activities) brings major benefits in physical and mental health, longevity, and well-being. Scientific studies of the benefits of exercise show that regular activity improves mood, reduces anxiety and depression, relieves stress, and improves memory (Blumenthal 2015). These activities—if we stay present, rather than on autopilot, while doing them—also help shift our attention from what's going on in our minds and into our body and direct experience.

  Moreover, research has shown the benefits of getting outside for relieving stress. A report that gathered evidence from 140 studies involving 290 million people on the effects of living close to nature and spending time outside showed a wide variety of health benefits, including reduced diastolic blood pressure, heart rate, and stress (University of East Anglia 2018).

- *Sleep, rest, naps, and slowing down:* As most of us know from our own experience, getting poor or insufficient sleep is a recipe for unhappiness and unease. Studies show that sleep is among the most critical factors for peak performance, memory, productivity, immune function, and mood regulation (Levitin 2016). Lack of sleep and poor sleep also create conditions that are not conducive to dealing well with stressors that arise.

  Cultivating habits that support healthy sleep (for example, dealing with stress mindfully during the day so as to be relaxed enough to sleep easily) as well as healthy sleep habits (such as getting sufficient sleep, having a regular bedtime, having a regular rising time, and so forth) are key to dealing mindfully with stress. Napping, which supports the recalibration of emotional equilibrium, has also been shown to reduce the incidence of cardiovascular disease, diabetes, stroke, and heart attack (Levitin 2016).

- *Nutritious diet:* Cultivating healthy habits of consumption, which we'll explore in chapter 8, helps create the conditions to respond more effectively to stressors that arise. When we are feeling nourished, alive, and engaged, we are well placed to respond flexibly and creatively to difficulties and challenges that arise. On the other hand, when we eat unconsciously, we not only create the conditions for poor physical and mental health outcomes, we also set ourselves up for increased stress and other poor health and life choices.

What are the ways you deal with stress? Which of your ways of responding to or relieving stress are helpful to you in the long run? What healthy habits would you like to develop to work wisely and compassionately with the stress in your life?

CHAPTER 8

Mindfulness and Our Habits of Consumption

Eat food. Not too much. Mostly plants.

—Michael Pollan, *The Omnivore's Dilemma*

Tatiana, a student who had attended one of my workshops, heard I was writing a book on mindfulness and habit change and shared how mindfulness had helped her transform her painful relationship with food: "Most evenings, while at the office or riding home, I would tell myself I'd really earned a good, full meal. I'd run to the grocery store and buy French fries and *lots* of cheese. By the time I got home, my blood sugar level was so low I'd start eating right away, finishing a block of cheese before dinner. I prepared the food hurriedly, wanting to eat as quickly as possible. I'd eat watching TV, totally disconnected from my body. After the meal I'd feel too full to move, so I'd watch TV until it was time for bed, where I couldn't sleep for hours. I'd get angry at myself for not taking care of my chores and how senseless life seemed! Next morning I'd tell myself in a stern and unloving voice: *Today you will do better.* Of course, I never managed…"

Tatiana's journey to living a more conscious life took effort, awareness, and kindness toward herself. She quit her high-powered job and found a less demanding one: "On my way home it took a lot of strength not to go into the grocery store. Often I'd walk in, stand there, and either buy some chewing gum or walk out without buying anything. When I got home, I had a ritual: make tea, eat a few olives, sit down at the table, and calm myself down with deep breathing and soothing words to myself: *You are safe.*

"It took a lot of effort to change. I found support in friends and loved ones, and I took refuge in nature, poems, art, literature, and my spiritual practice. It's been five years, and I only rarely slip back into my old habit. As I brought mindfulness to my eating habits, I connected with my underlying beliefs—I felt I didn't deserve to look after myself and that nobody would care about me anyway. These beliefs are still with me but are now held in a sea of understanding and love. I honor them by providing spiritual food—giving myself what I really need. When I lapse, I respond now with kindness and a renewed commitment not to go back. I have come to see this eating pattern as a lamp that is showing me where I have veered off my path, when I am not looking after myself enough in other areas of my life."

Tatiana's story may sound familiar to many of us. We often eat and drink in ways that don't make us happy, feeling like we're on autopilot, wishing it were different but not knowing where to start or how to change. Our habits of consumption—what we take into our body, mind, and spirit—affect our quality of life, longevity, capacity for happiness, and ultimately our freedom. Our habits of consumption cause us stress and harm when they remain unconscious and disconnected from how we want to live. And they can be a source of happiness and peace when our true aspirations and our behavior are in alignment.

As was the case for Tatiana, mindfulness helps us to see when we are acting unconsciously in ways that harm us and are out of alignment with our deepest aspirations. It also supports us in establishing new and more helpful habits.

Bringing Mindfulness to Habits of Consumption

In this chapter we'll look at how we can make our habits work for us by aligning our behavior with our values and intentions—consciously cultivating habits that enhance well-being and happiness. We'll pay particular attention to food because all of us must eat to survive, yet our habits of eating can be a cause of unhappiness and suffering. We'll also touch on other habits of consumption—including drinking alcohol, smoking, and using drugs—as well as the way we take in information. We'll look at how mindfulness can help disentangle us from these unhealthy habits and cultivate wiser and healthier ones.

The extent of the social and human costs of unhealthy habits of consumption—particularly related to eating, smoking, and drinking alcohol—can be seen in nationwide U.S. statistics:

- 61 percent of Americans are overweight or obese—on average, American men and women gained seventeen and nineteen pounds, respectively, between the late 1970s and 2009 (Pollan 2009).

- An estimated twenty million women and ten million men in the United States will have an eating disorder at some time in their lives (Mirasol 2018).

- 33 million Americans are "problem drinkers," and an estimated 36 percent of men have struggled with problem drinking in their lives (Associated Press 2015a; Associated Press 2015b).

- 38 million American adults smoked cigarettes "every day" or "some days" in 2016, and smoking causes 480,000 deaths a year in the United States (CDC 2018; CDC 2019).

The problem with unhealthy habits of consumption extends far beyond those who have an addiction or disorder, or who seek professional help. Many of us have, or have had, a sticky and difficult relationship with food, drink, tobacco, or other drugs. Do you find yourself caught up in any of the following habits?

- Snacking on sweets during the day to deal with boredom, anxiety, or stress

- Eating more—or less—than what is healthy because you feel needy or unloved, or because you are trying to conform to a mental image of how you should look

- Drinking alcohol every evening as a means of dealing with the stress of work

- Smoking cigarettes as a way to relieve stress or agitation, or as a habit accompanying many daily activities

- Taking in information on the Internet, TV, or other media to stay informed—but doing it in a way that makes you more stressed, angry, or overwhelmed

- Shopping to comfort yourself or address other emotional needs rather than purchasing what you actually need

- Taking a recreational drug habitually to numb the pain of daily life

In all these examples, we are in automatic mode—pulled along by the weight of our past actions and often triggered by environmental cues. Our habits are in the driver's seat, and we are acting them out largely unconsciously. Our behavior is out of alignment with our true needs—what we are taking in is not what will do us good but more often is a way to avoid painful or unpleasant feelings.

If we want to be genuinely happy and free from the stress and worry that accompany these unconscious habits, we need to align our behavior with what truly nurtures us—and with our deepest aspirations for ourselves and our lives. Mindfulness is a flashlight that can help us identify where the problem lies and point out the direction we need to go in.

So how can we bring our behaviors back into alignment with our aspirations and untangle ourselves from unhealthy habits of consumption? We begin where we are by acknowledging the truth of what is happening and by connecting with our deepest intentions. We do this by using the five-step habit-transformation practice introduced in chapter 5, with some modifications:

1. Recognize the need to change a habit

2. Cultivate the intention to make a change

3. Deepen your awareness of the habit

4. Develop strategies and approaches to help change a habit

5. Make a specific plan and repeat the behavior

1. Recognize the need to change a habit

For many of us, our unhealthy habits involving food, drink, and other indulgences are clear and obvious—we know that a particular habit (for example, snacking unconsciously, or drinking more glasses of wine in the evening than feels wise, or smoking cigarettes) is not what we really want to be doing. We may question whether we have the capacity to change the habit, or if this is the best time to try, or if it's worth the effort it will take. But we are clear that our behavior is out of alignment with our deeper intentions—and we can explore our intention to make a change.

For others of us, it may not be so clear that anything needs to change. In this case, it may help to sit quietly in meditation or reflection and bring awareness to what (food, drink, other substances, information, and so forth) and how we consume. We can reflect on our behaviors and see if any activity we regularly engage in causes stress, tension, discomfort, or other difficult feelings, sensations, thoughts, or emotions. If we become aware of a harmful habit, we can then explore our commitment to making a change.

No matter the level of awareness of your habits, if you've identified a habit that's limiting you or causing stress or harm, ask yourself, *Is this habit calling for my committed attention and effort? Is this something I need to change?* If it is, you can connect with your intention to change the habit. Then you can get to know the habit more intimately and, most importantly, without judgment.

2. Cultivate the intention to make a change

Take some time to reflect on your intention to make a change. Sit quietly, relaxing your body and allowing yourself to be fully present. Ask yourself, *What is my heartfelt intention for myself and for my life, my deepest wish and aspiration?*

Pause to take in whatever response comes up. It might be peace, joy, happiness, or love… Or a vision of yourself living happily… If it's difficult to connect with your deepest intention or there is resistance, you might ask yourself, *What am I believing right now? What, if anything, am I holding on to? What is the barrier to me fully understanding my intention?*

Then, ask yourself, *How does the habit that I've identified get in the way of living out my deepest intention?* Again, sit and meet with kindness whatever comes up... Perhaps, tightness, tension, judgment, or shame...

Then ask yourself, *How important is it for me to change this habit? How committed am I to making a change?* Stay connected to your deepest intention—your commitment to make a change in the habit you've identified—and come back regularly to your intention as you implement the practices we discuss in this chapter.

Then imagine or envision how you might feel in, say, two or three months when you've let go of this unhealthy habit, reduced its frequency, or developed a more helpful behavior. Allow yourself to experience whatever bodily sensations, feelings, or emotions come up as you reflect on the benefits of making this change.

If your commitment is strong and you are inspired by the potential benefits of making this change, reflect on strategies to make a change. Begin by writing down the benefits you envision from changing this habit or naming the barriers to locating this intention.

3. Deepen your awareness of the habit

The more familiar you are with how the habit gets enacted, the more you are in a position to be mindful and strategic in making helpful changes. You might journal your responses to these questions to gain a better awareness of your habits:

Who are you with?

Where are you when carrying out this habit?

When do you do it?

How do you feel at the time?

How do you feel later?

What does this habit provide you with?

How does this habit limit you or stop you from enjoying life?

What is the deeper need that underlies this habit?

Is there another activity you could replace this habit with, limit the extent to which you engage in it, or become more conscious of it for when you are ready to make a change?

The more familiar we are with the habit pattern, the more we can work wisely and kindly to make a change. A necessary step to making helpful change is to cultivate a clear intention to bring attention to the habit, be willing to open to whatever feelings arise, and choose a wiser and more helpful response.

4. Develop strategies and approaches to help change a habit

It can be helpful to think about a habit beyond just the moment you are carrying it out. You can reflect on what leads up to the behavior (*before*); the immediate triggers, urges, context, and feelings (*during*); and what follows afterward (*after*). Let's take the habit of eating sweets unconsciously in the evening as a means of relieving stress at the end of a long day.

- *Before*: Think about what you might do before the habit arises to make it less likely or tempting. For example, when shopping you might consciously choose not to purchase sweets and only buy healthy snacks that are more aligned to what your body needs.

- *During*: When you feel the pull of the habit (for example, at home in the evening), consciously bring awareness to what you are feeling and experiencing (bodily sensations, emotions, thoughts) and choose to stay with the feelings. Ride the waves of uncomfortable sensations when they arise, and ask yourself, *What would be a wise and healthy way of responding to these feelings and urges now?* You might simply stay with the feelings, letting them come and go, or choose to eat a nourishing snack, meditate, take a walk, or another beneficial response.

- *After*: If you have succumbed to the habit, choose to meet any judgments or feelings of self-blame or disappointment with compassion toward yourself. Then recommit to choosing a more helpful response next time.

Additionally, inquire into an obstacle that might arise to changing this habit. Research shows that thinking in advance about a temptation or challenge to maintaining a positive habit, and contemplating how you would address it, is a powerful support for successful change (Quinn et al. 2010). For example, if you drink too much when you go out with colleagues after work, imagine how you would respond if asked to join them for a few beers.

Another key to changing unhelpful habits is to make the new helpful behaviors easier to do—and make those unwanted habits harder to do or less obvious. James Clear (2018), who has written extensively on habit change, provides a fourfold approach: Make unhelpful habits *invisible*, *unattractive*, *difficult*, and *unsatisfying*—and make helpful habits you want to cultivate more *obvious*, *attractive*, *easy*, and *satisfying*.

For example, if you want to exercise more regularly, leave your running shoes in a visible place by the door (*obvious*). If you want to stop smoking, think about the smell of tobacco on your clothes, or how it feels to wake up with a smoker's cough (*unattractive*). If you want to be more mindful in daily life, use everyday cues—such as the phone ringing or mealtimes—as an opportunity to consciously pause for a few mindful moments (*easy*). If you want to develop a habit of taking regular walks in nature, think about how pleasant it will be to feel your body moving, hear the sounds of birds, feel the breeze on your face (*satisfying*).

5. Make a specific plan and repeat the behavior

When you prepare well and then repeat your actions often enough, it becomes habitual. As noted earlier, research shows that the more we specify the steps we will take to break or develop a habit, the more likely we are to succeed. These are known as *implementation intentions*. For example, you might decide: *Whenever I have a judgmental thought about myself, I will consciously wish myself well.* Then repeat the actions until the habit becomes automatic (Gollwitzer and Schaal 1998).

It helps to write down your commitment, share it with a friend or loved one, commit to doing it for a set period (for example, one week), and check off each day you complete the behavior. At the end of the set time make a new commitment for a similar period.

You can use this approach with a variety of habits that you wish to change: quitting smoking, changing your relationship to alcohol and recreational drugs, modifying your patterns of consuming information, stopping unconscious spending, and more.

You can ask, *How important is it to make this change? How strong is my intention to make a change? When, where, why, and with whom am I when I act out this habit? What practices and approaches help me before, during, and after? What can make it easier or more obvious to cultivate a new habit? What makes it more difficult or less obvious to let go of an old one?*

In a spirit of compassion and curiosity, you can then commit to developing the new habit or letting go of the old one for a set period. And then commit again, until the behavior has become habitual.

Cultivating a Wise Relationship with Consumption

What we take into our body, mind, and spirit—and how we do so—has a great impact on our health and well-being and on the lives of other humans, animals, and the planet. Bringing greater awareness to what we consume can contribute to our own health and happiness, as well as to the alleviation of suffering of others.

Much of our consumption is unconscious. We eat and drink and consume the way we do because we grew up habituated to these behaviors. Our society, organized around these forms of production and consumption, naturally presents these practices and habits as the norm—and few of us take the time and effort to examine whether our habits contribute to our own well-being. We rarely look behind the curtain at the conditions under which our food comes to our plate.

Our Western diet—consisting mainly of processed foods and meat; refined grains; high amounts of sugar and fat; and relatively little fruit, vegetables, and whole grains—contributes to high rates of obesity, cardiovascular diseases, and cancer (Pollan 2009). This diet also contributes to the suffering of many other sentient creatures that are raised in painful and inhumane conditions.

Around 11 billion animals are raised and killed for meat, eggs, and milk in the United States, including a million chickens killed every hour (HSUS n.d.). Livestock are also responsible for 18 percent of the greenhouse gas emissions that contribute to climate change—as much as all trucks and cars. And millions of square miles of forests, which are natural carbon "sinks," have been cut to graze livestock (Worldwatch n.d.; HSUS n.d.).

When we choose to bring awareness to our habits of consumption, rather than beating ourselves up or feeling guilty, which tend not to be helpful responses, we can explore with compassion their impact and the choices we might make that support our own and others' well-being. Beginning with bringing awareness to the food you eat, you might explore these ideas and ask yourself what steps, if any, you might take for your own and others' well-being.

Here are some ways you can bring awareness to what you eat:

- Eat a diet that is primarily plant based—rich in vegetables and fruits.

- Where possible, eat organic and locally grown food.

- Limit or avoid consumption of meat.

- If you drink alcohol, consume it with awareness and in moderation.

- Make a commitment to learning about the effects of your choices on yourself, others, and the earth. Ask yourself, *Are there steps I can take to contribute to my own health and well-being while bringing awareness to the conditions of those producing my food, lessening the suffering of animals, and limiting the impact on the earth?*

Here are ways you can eat with awareness:

- Eat when you are hungry. Ask, *Why am I eating?*

- Connect with your feelings rather than responding to external cues.

- Focus on quality over quantity.

- Slow down and pay attention, putting aside other activities.

- Bring awareness to times when you eat unconsciously (for example, when anxious or bored). Ask, *What would be a more helpful response now?*

- Prepare your own meals as much as possible.

Are there other things you can do to bring greater consciousness to what you eat and drink—to give yourself what your body, mind, and spirit really need? Are there choices that you might make that would be conducive to better health for you, minimize harm, and contribute to others' well-being? And, whatever you do, can you do it with kindness and compassion for yourself and everyone else who is caught up in a system that is much larger than ourselves—and do all this with integrity and without finger-wagging and beating yourself up?

Unconscious and unwise consumption are a source of suffering for many. Mindfulness provides skills to recognize when our consumption of food, drink, or other substances is causing us harm and to make wiser and healthier choices— for our own benefit and for the well-being of other creatures and the earth.

CHAPTER 9

Mindfulness of Devices and Distractions

Like many in high-stress jobs, Chapin, a student in my meditation class who calls himself "a compulsive email checker and phone reacher," has the habit of constantly reaching for his phone to check messages. When there's a pause in the conversation or move from one location to another, he reaches for his phone. He hears the refrain in his head, *Has something appeared in my inbox that needs immediate attention? Am I missing out on something?*

Chapin relayed a story of how on a trip to the West Coast he had been a "model of mindfulness" until the flight home. Then, "Something dreadful occurred," he said. "The Wi-Fi on the plane wasn't working! Oh, the horror! Think of all the important emails that were flooding my inbox while I was 30,000 feet in the air!"

He'd packed my book, *The Here-and-Now Habit*, with him. Unable to lean on his familiar laptop crutch, he dug into the book and spent some time meditating on where this impulse was coming from and the broader story that had him caught up so often.

"As we were starting our descent, I paid close attention to what I was feeling: anxious anticipation, *leaning into the future*... Once on the ground, I noted the sensations in my body: the rapid heartbeat, the tug to do, do, do... But I didn't reach for my phone. I let the feelings come and go. Only after I was settled at home, did I open my laptop. Surprise! The world had kept on spinning while I was in the air and nothing urgent was waiting for me.

"Since then, I've tried to be 'compassionately curious' about what I'm feeling and experiencing when I default to unhelpful habits. This has given me a critical pause to judge whether an action is necessary and then act with intention.

"It's made a tremendous difference in my life. Addressing my habits is much more doable now. I feel empowered to observe my habits and alter their course in real time. That's a wonderful gift and has helped me engage more mindfully in conversation with my wife (catching that impulse to criticize or rebut), my children (being able to choose patience when I feel it slipping away), and my colleagues (particularly, when things get heated)."

Working Skillfully with Technology

As Chapin can attest, the amount of information available to us daily and the speed of its delivery is extraordinary. It also provides profound challenges to our balance and well-being. We are walking around with devices in our pockets and purses containing the equivalent of half a million books. In 2011, Americans took in five times as much information as they did in 1986: 100,000 words every day, the equivalent of 175 newspapers (Levitin 2016).

Unsurprisingly, information—news stories, emails, social media posts, films, games, sports, and other media—are delivered to us in enticing ways, with sounds and alerts designed to trigger our reward systems with the buzz of getting a few more likes for our Facebook post, a text from a friend or loved one, or almost winning in a video game.

We all appreciate the benefits of being able to instantly see and communicate with someone on the other side of the world or having the latest information in real time wherever we are. But our brain and nervous system evolved thousands of years ago to deal with a very different environment—one where we might meet one thousand people in our entire life-time and rarely travel more than a few miles from our place of birth. We are ill-equipped for our current information-drenched environment.

It shouldn't come as a shock that many of us are paying a high price for unhealthy habits related to our consumption of technology, as well as for our relationship to our phones and other devices. In this chapter, we'll discuss the problematic habits linked to our relationship to technology and devices; explore and practice skills of mindfulness that can help us achieve a healthy relationship with technology; and outline some helpful strategies for cultivating awareness and organizing our lives to live more wisely.

The Challenges of Technology and Devices

The challenges of the exponential growth in power, speed, and ubiquity of technology and the devices that put information into our hands 24/7 easily leads us into unhealthy habits that negatively affect our quality of life.

These harmful habits can take the form of behavioral addictions. In his book *Irresistible: The Rise of Addictive Technology and the Business of Keeping Us Hooked*, Adam Alter (2017) highlights studies that suggest that 41 percent of the population has suffered at least one behavioral addiction in the previous twelve months. He also reports that 48 percent of a sample of university students were "Internet addicts"—and another 40 percent were borderline or potential addicts. Studies cited by Nancy Colier (2016) in her book *The Power of Off* labeled Twitter and Facebook as more addictive than smoking or alcohol; and research on millennials found that half of them would rather give up their sense of smell than abandon a critical device like their smartphone!

Even short of behavioral addiction, many of us have harmful habitual ways of engaging with technology and our devices. Phone use has risen from an average of eighteen minutes a day in 2008 to two hours and forty-eight minutes in 2015 (Alter 2017). And we spend an average of almost one hundred hours a month checking email, texting, playing games, surfing the web, reading articles, and so forth—amounting to eleven years over an average lifetime (Alter 2017).

Like Chapin, many of us are familiar with the habit energy of wanting to check our phone to get a momentary buzz of relief or excitement. Otherwise we feel as if we are missing something or getting behind. We know that there is a cost in terms of our focus on what needs to be done and our relationship with loved ones or work colleagues—yet, we are still pulled toward the largely unconscious behavior.

Distraction—any interruption that causes someone to stop what they are doing—has a high cost in terms of stress and effectiveness. A case study of email use in a medium-size company found that employees reacted to a new email within six seconds of its arrival, and that it took an average of sixty-four seconds to recover and return to their work (Jackson et al. 2003).

The Myth of Multitasking

In order to deal with the pressures and stresses of modern life (such as responding to deadlines, being available at any time due to the ubiquity of technology, trying to juggle responsibilities in the workplace and at home), many of us try to multitask. We give just sufficient attention to one task before shifting our attention to another urgent priority. Sometimes we think we are pretty good at doing this; at other times we feel overwhelmed. But the truth, shown in numerous research studies, is that multitasking is a myth for almost all of us.

Studies show that multitasking increases stress levels, can cause short-term memory loss, and reduces our ability to filter relevant from irrelevant information (Blumenthal 2015). We take 50 percent longer to perform a task when interrupted and make 50 percent more errors (Blumenthal 2015, citing Rogers and Monsell 1995). And a study that tested students' ability to drive while responding by phone to a task involving mental concentration found that only one in forty (2.5 percent) was a successful multitasker (Watson and Strayer 2010)!

In his book *The Organized Mind*, Daniel Levitin (2016, 306) quotes Stanford professor Clifford Nass's conclusion about multitasking:

> It turns out multitaskers are terrible at every aspect of multitasking. They're terrible at ignoring irrelevant information; they're terrible at keeping information in their head… and they're terrible at switching from one task to another.

Five Steps to Healthy Tech Habits

Mindfulness is an effective way to cultivate a healthy relationship with our phones, devices, and technology, so that we can live *with* technology rather than feeling we have to unplug from it completely or be swept up in its energies and demands. As we've emphasized earlier, unhealthy habits become automatic and unconscious through repetition. Mindfulness helps us to bring the unconscious and automatic behaviors into awareness so that we can make more helpful and skillful choices.

Mindfulness puts us back in the driver's seat on a *macro* level—allowing us to recognize the overall habit (for example, constantly checking our emails, texts, and so forth) and see that it has real costs in terms of stress, effectiveness, and our relationships. Mindfulness also gives us control on a *micro* level—inviting us to cultivate the skills to work moment by moment with the habit energies that keep us stuck in unconscious and unhelpful habits.

We can use the five-step habit-transformation approach highlighted in previous chapters, focusing here on an unconscious and unhealthy relationship with our devices, texts, emails, social media, games, and so on.

1. Recognize the need to change a habit

Bring awareness to the unconscious and habitual ways you use your devices (for example, checking for texts or emails, moving from one Internet site to another, and so on). Ask yourself, *Is this a habit I need to give attention to? What impact is it having on my focus, effectiveness, and relationships? How would changing this habit allow me to live with less stress and greater ease?*

2. Cultivate the intention to make a change

If this is a behavior you would like to change, check in on the seriousness of your intention. Is this something you are willing to put effort into over time to let go of the habit and cultivate another way of responding to its triggers and urges? How would it feel to have successfully made this change? Take in any feelings that arise.

State your intention in words and write it down. For example, *My intention is to change my relationship with my phone, so that I use it when necessary—to take care of work projects and keep in touch with loved ones and friends—rather than as a crutch. I commit to bringing awareness to my underlying feelings when I have the urge to check email and text messages. I will take steps to make it easier and more obvious to make the healthier choice when I become aware of the urge to go online, check Facebook, and so on.*

3. Deepen your awareness of the habit

Become familiar with the contexts—the who, what, when, where, and why—in which the habit arises. Do you go to your phone unconsciously at work, at home, or everywhere? Do you do it when you are with family, friends, or colleagues? More at certain times of day than other times? What feelings do you notice just before you move your attention to your phone or other device? What thoughts are you aware of?

Ask yourself, *What would I have to experience* (for example, anxiety or boredom) *if I didn't check my email right now?* Notice how it feels to stay with the feelings rather than avoiding them by checking your phone.

4. Develop strategies and approaches to help change a habit

Ask yourself:

- *What can I do to make it easier for myself to break the habit of incessantly checking my phone for updates and news? What can I do to make the device less obvious and easier to resist?* Some steps include putting the phone in a specific place in the house and only using it for a particular purpose and then returning it to its place. (We'll consider more strategies below.)

- *What will I do if I feel the urge to check my phone?* Commit to choosing to stay with the feelings you're experiencing. Ride the waves of any challenging feelings and emotions, knowing that they only last a limited time.

- *When I've been surfing the Internet mindlessly for an hour and I start beating myself up for being unfocused and lazy, how will I respond?* Commit to forgiving yourself. Then renew your commitment to the helpful habit and begin again. There will be lapses in your journey to creating healthier habits. Treat yourself with kindness when that happens.

- *What situation would pull me into unconscious Internet surfing or social media scrolling?* Common culprits are when we are tired, worried, or bored. How do you envision responding in this situation?

5. Make a specific plan and repeat the behavior

Commit to building a new relationship with your phone, TV, other device, or technology use in general over the next week. Write down your commitment as clearly and specifically as possible. For example, "I will commit to only checking email and responding to messages once in the morning and once in the afternoon for thirty minutes."

Reflect on how things are going at different times in the day—are there any adjustments that would be helpful? At the end of the day, check off your completion and any lessons or insights. Think about times when you lapsed and how you might do things differently next time. Continue the process each day, taking time to appreciate your effort and the benefits that come with this change.

Organizing Our Days Mindfully

For some, the difficulty of engaging with technology and the flood of information coming in may lead us to choose a more simple life and thus get off the grid. For most of us, though, this may not be an option—our work and family life may require us to be online; our digital connections may be obligatory. But with mindfulness—and continued diligence—we can develop a wise relationship to technology and our devices. We can use technology while staying in the driver's seat and not being swept up, addicted, or overwhelmed.

One key support for developing healthy habits around our devices and technology is to pay close attention to how we are organizing our days and our life. I'll suggest here some tips that I've learned from my own challenges with organizing my life and my days—I could focus on a project and do it well, but I found it difficult to juggle and prioritize different tasks and responsibilities. At times this resulted in stress and anxiety, as I worried about how I would be able to get everything done and what would happen if I didn't.

I found mindfulness and self-compassion to be essential to working with the challenges arising from lack of organization—particularly in helping work with challenging thoughts and emotions. Finding and developing tools and skills to mindfully organize my day and my life were also indispensable. For example, I found that Bullet Journaling (which I call "mindful journaling") helped me link my daily tasks and goals with my longer-range vision and priorities. With a simple notebook and a straightforward methodology, I can take care of my daily responsibilities and tasks while keeping my eyes on the prize—staying focused on longer-term goals and aspirations. I'm much less stressed and have had the opportunity to make changes that have helped bring more ease and effectiveness to my life.

Here are some guidelines that I have found useful:

Ways to organize your day and your time:

- Work for a set period on a specific task or project—say fifty to sixty minutes, long enough to focus and concentrate on a task. Commit to not interrupting yourself, for example, by checking your phone, during this period.

- Break up large tasks into smaller chunks and focus on one chunk at a time.

- Set specific times for email and social media—say, thirty minutes in the morning and thirty minutes in the afternoon or evening. Consider not checking or using email or social media outside those times unless there is something crucial to attend to.

- Turn off email and social media alerts so that your attention isn't constantly being pulled away from what you are working on.

- Put your phone out of sight, perhaps in another room, so that you won't be tempted to check emails, texts, or social media.

- Take breaks that allow you to move out of focused mode—letting your mind rest, wander, and make unexpected connections.

- Don't underestimate the power of a good nap: fifteen, twenty, or thirty minutes. A ten-minute nap can be equivalent to an extra hour and a half of sleep at night (Levitin 2016).

Move information out of your brain and into the environment:

- Have places where things routinely go, so you don't have to think about them or look for them (for example, keys in a basket by the door, phone on a side table).

- Use the environment to remind you of what you need to do (such as putting your running shoes by the door to remind you to jog after work).

- Write down things you need to do or remember so that you are not constantly trying to hold everything in your mind.

- Write down goals—individuals who documented their goals are on average 33 percent more successful in accomplishing them (Blumenthal 2015).

- Have different spaces for different tasks, types of work, and other activity.

Give up the illusion of multitasking:

- Ask yourself, *What is it most important for me to be doing now?* Focus on this for a set period, knowing that this is what you need to be doing right now. When your mind is drawn to a distraction, remember your intention and stay focused.

- Build your capacity to focus on one task by focusing for twenty minutes the first day, thirty minutes the second day, and so on until you can focus for sixty to ninety minutes.

In addition to these mindful steps to organize, we can practice bringing mindfulness to those moments when we feel pulled into unhealthy habits of relating to technology and devices. We can ask ourselves: *What would I have to experience if I do not to check my phone, social media, and the like?* Then choose to stay with those feelings, riding the waves of uncomfortable bodily sensations or emotions, and see that they come and go. And choose, if appropriate, a more skillful response (for example, taking a five-minute stretch break). We can also come back and reflect on our intentions and ask, *What is most important right now? What will contribute to genuine happiness and well-being?*

Our devices and the information available to us 24/7 can be a source of suffering and disconnection from ourselves, others, and our lives. With mindfulness, we can develop a more skillful relationship with devices and technology, allowing us to use them with awareness rather than being controlled by them.

CHAPTER 10

Mindfulness and Habits of Speech and Communication

Speech can break lives, create enemies, and start wars, or it can give wisdom, heal divisions, and create peace.

—Bhikkhu Bodhi, *The Noble Eightfold Path*

During the American civil rights movement, Rev. Dr. Martin Luther King Jr. said to segregationists in the South, "I've seen too much hate to want to hate... Do to us what you will and we will still love you... and one day we will win our freedom. We will not only win freedom for ourselves; we will appeal to your heart and conscience... and our victory will be a double victory." The commitment of Dr. King and the movement of nonviolence in words and action played a major role in the advances in civil rights in the 1950s and 1960s.

There are many other historical examples of speech being used to build harmony and reconciliation. But speech has also been used to create division and hatred, from Nazi Germany to the Rwandan genocide to the United States' treatment of vulnerable minorities.

Communication is a central area of our lives—one that is linked closely to our most intimate relationships and fundamental needs. How we speak and what we say influence whether collectively we live together harmoniously or in conflict. Our speech leads to joy and sorrow, pleasure and pain, connection and separation, happiness and suffering—for ourselves and others. Bringing greater awareness to our habits of speech—and the beliefs, emotions, and feelings that trigger or support our communication—is a key area of our life to give attention to.

Pause and reflect on your own speech: verbal and nonverbal, emails, text messages, other written communications, social media, gestures, songs, poetry, talks, and so forth. Is there a particular way you communicate or a specific content of your speech that gets you in trouble or makes you feel remorseful? Or that you'd like to change? For example:

> Do you get frustrated with representatives on the phone when you have difficulty getting what you need from a company—and speak in an annoyed tone to them?

Do you speak angrily to a spouse, partner, or family member when they don't act in ways that you like?

Do you tell lies or partial truths when you are asked about something that might lower you in the eyes of others?

Do you share gossip or information with a friend about a third person to put that person down or feel a bond of closeness with your friend?

Do you pad your résumé to present an elevated but inaccurate picture of yourself to prospective employers?

Do you speak angrily or judgmentally about political figures and help create an echo chamber of disagreement with those whose views and policies you oppose?

On the other hand, are there instances when you feel good about what you say and how you say it—when your words are intended to cultivate harmony and connection, and help you to feel engaged and at ease?

It can be the work of a lifetime to cultivate wise and kind speech—and abandon harmful habits of communication. I've found two approaches particularly helpful in exploring our habits of communication: the Buddha's teachings on wise and appropriate speech, and Marshall

Rosenberg's Nonviolent Communication (NVC). The Buddha's teachings focus on our intentions, the content of our speech, and its effect on ourselves, others, and the world. NVC emphasizes a more relational approach to speech, focusing on the needs that underlie our words and how all parties can work to have their needs met. These two approaches provide skills and practices to help us to:

- Cultivate wise and kind speech

- Abandon harmful kinds of communication

- Meet our own needs while helping others meet theirs

The Buddha's Teaching on Wise Speech

For the Buddha, living 2,500 years ago in a society of mainly oral communication, cultivating wise and harmonious speech was both a way to "purify the mind" and attain the greatest freedom in this human life. It was also viewed as a skill to help people live together in harmony rather than in strife. The Buddha's teachings on wise speech are normally framed in terms of four instructions on what to avoid—but contained in the instructions are also positive qualities of communication to cultivate while abstaining from false speech, slanderous speech, harsh speech, and idle chatter.

Abstaining from False Speech

This means never to lie—not for our own benefit or to harm anyone else. Speaking the truth is essential to living together in a way that invites mutual trust. And key to speaking the truth lies in our intention—in not intending to deceive another. When we lie, we cause harm to others and society by undermining trust in each other.

We also cause harm to ourselves—creating division and separation within ourselves and needing to lie again to cover up or embellish the earlier lie. We separate ourselves from the truth—in the Buddha's teachings this is the exact opposite of freedom, which is found by taking refuge in the truth (dharma). In the words of Bhikkhu Bodhi, "[T]ruthful speech is a matter of taking our stand on reality rather than illusion" (2000, 50).

We can see the price we pay for false speech in the harm that is caused to the social fabric of trust when political leaders spread falsehoods and conspiracy theories, knowing they are not true.

Abstaining from Slanderous Speech

This is speech that is intended to create enmity and alienate one person or group from another. It is most often motivated by anger or hatred and intended to harm. The opposite of slanderous speech is communication that promotes harmony and friendship.

Abstaining from Harsh Speech

Harsh speech means angry, hurtful, insulting, abusive, or offensive speech. The main root of harsh speech is anger and aversion. Its opposite is kind, friendly, and agreeable speech. We see in the political rhetoric of the late 2010s the damage and harm that come from these three forms of unwise speech: lies being presented wholesale as the truth, and division and hostility being fomented for political and personal gain.

Abstaining from Idle Chatter

This encompasses pointless talk that lacks thought and purpose. Much of our speech when we are unconscious, unmindful, or careless with our words can be harmful to ourselves and others in cultivating a mind that is not at ease or clear—and encouraging others to develop such states. Think of the ways we can be lazy in our speech, or fill up space in the conversation just to avoid discomfort or anxiety, and how this easily leads to gossip and unwise language. As the old proverb says, "The devil still some mischief finds for idle hands [and minds] to do."

These days, pointless talk also includes much that passes for entertainment. The opposite, positive quality is being thoughtful and conscious in our speech and sharing only what is true, kind, necessary, and appropriate.

These four kinds of speech—framed both negatively and positively—cover most of the harmful and beneficial kinds of speech in our daily lives, for example:

- Getting defensive with your partner because you feel as if you're being criticized, and then responding with an angry remark

- Sending a note of gratitude to a friend who brought you soup when you were sick

- Talking harshly and critically about your boss to a colleague

- Calling to congratulate a colleague who has received an award at work

In meditation, as well as in our daily lives, the Buddha's teachings on wise speech provide skills to work with the roots of harmful communication habits and to develop kind and thoughtful ways of communicating. They help you to:

- Consciously cultivate the intention to be honest, careful, and kind in your speech, so that you don't create harm for yourself or others.

- Envision how you might respond wisely in situations where you feel strong emotions.

- Bring kind awareness to underlying thoughts, feelings, and emotions that give rise to unwise or unkind speech, and allow yourself to experience them, letting them come and go without acting them out in angry or impatient speech.

- Choose to cultivate loving-kindness, compassion, or forgiveness toward a person that brings up in you feelings of harsh judgment, anger, or blame.

- Acknowledge the harm you've caused when you've spoken in ways that are untrue, unkind, or unconscious—and hold yourself and anyone you have hurt with compassion—*and* commit to acting and speaking truthfully and kindly in the future.

Bringing Wise Attention to Your Speech

Pay attention to your speech for a period of time (for example, one morning or afternoon, or an entire day), including via emails and other written communications.

Stay as fully present as you can with your body, emotions, and thoughts when you are engaged in conversation or waiting your turn to speak. Commit to speaking with kindness and care. Remain present for the person with whom you are communicating.

Bring awareness to your intentions when you are about to speak or send a text or email. What do you notice? Tension?

Busyness? Annoyance? Kindness? See how it feels to hold back from speaking or sending a message if you are aware of anger, annoyance, or other energy that creates separation. Invite kindness and acceptance to what you are experiencing, and then let the feelings come and go...

What harmful habits of speech, if any, do you notice? How might you envision bringing more kindness and compassion to your communication. How can you deliver your words accompanied by the intention of kindness? Ask yourself periodically about your speech: *Is what I'm saying or writing true? Is it necessary? Kind? Timely?* Commit to communicating only in ways that contribute to your own and others' well-being and happiness.

Cultivating Wise and Kind Speech with NVC

Another approach to transforming our habits of communication is Nonviolent Communication, developed by Marshall Rosenberg. This framework provides an approach to help us meet our underlying needs while helping the person we're communicating with meet theirs.

NVC is a practice that is fundamentally grounded in awareness—of our own inner and outer experience and curiosity about and interest in the experience of the person with whom we are communicating. It also helps us bring awareness to the dance of our interaction and the wider context and relationships within which our communication is unfolding. Marshall Rosenberg said, "I developed NVC as a way to train my attention—to shine the light of consciousness—on places that have the potential to yield what I am seeking. What I want in my life is compassion, a flow between myself and others based on a mutual giving of the heart" (Sofer 2018, 73).

The NVC approach is rooted in an understanding that our speech is a way of getting our fundamental needs met. The more we attune to our own experience—our feelings, emotions, bodily sensations, thoughts—the more we are able to move toward knowing what we want most deeply. We're also then able to better identify ways of fulfilling that need. And the more we attune to and empathize with the experience of the person with whom we are communicating—their feelings, emotions, and underlying needs—the more we move in the direction of greater understanding and toward each of us getting our needs met. This understanding and approach helps contribute to living together with greater peace and harmony.

When we consciously include the practices of mindfulness, as Oren Sofer—a longtime mindfulness practitioner, mindfulness teacher, and NVC trainer—does in his book, *Say What You Mean: A Mindfulness Approach to Nonviolent Communication*, the NVC approach is further enriched. We can then transform unhelpful and unconscious habits into skills and practices of communication to meet our deepest human needs.

In summarizing key elements of NVC, we'll use this mindfulness approach to highlight ways we can fruitfully change our habits of communication.

The Four Steps of NVC

NVC provides a framework involving four key experiences to enhance our communication: *observations*, *feelings*, *needs*, and *requests*. Sofer (2018, 110) reframes these as questions: "What happened? How do you feel about it? Why? And where do we go from here?" I've reframed them as steps you can take for making skillful and kind communication a habit:

1. Speak in the language of observations.

Avoid making judgments or evaluations. Rather than telling a friend who's late for a meeting that "You're always late," you might let them know with kindness that "This is the third time you've arrived more than fifteen minutes after the time we said we'd meet." When you speak in the specific and objective language of observations, it's easier for the other person to hear, since they are less likely to feel as if they're being accused or judged. In this way, communication is based on an understanding of what actually happened.

For many of us, it isn't our default to speak in terms of observations, particularly in situations of conflict or difference. And it isn't always easy to move from reactivity or defensiveness to observation. With mindfulness, you can build the capacity to work with your own reactions—emotions, bodily feelings, and mental stories—with kindness. With mindfulness, you can use these skills to find a way back to what happened and how to share your experience with the other person.

2. Express what you are feeling.

When you express what you are feeling (for example, "I felt sad last night when you told me you wanted to go out and spend time with friends, because I was hoping we could spend some time together"), you are sharing your direct experience rather than blaming or attacking. Compare this to: "You never stay home with me. You'd always rather be with your friends." The first example allows space for dialogue, while the second invites defensiveness and reactivity.

When you open to your emotions, you can see them as providing important information, rather than being something bad that's happening that you have to act out or suppress. Your emotions tell you that what's happening matters. They are a way in which you express your needs. For instance, your sadness may tell you that you're looking for connection, intimacy, warmth, or another need.

When you open to your emotions without fear and bring compassionate curiosity to what you're feeling (for example, pulsing, warmth, stories, emotions), the energy moves through you more freely. This helps you connect with what you are needing in this moment or situation. Sharing with the other person what you are feeling (for instance, "When you came home after midnight, I felt sad…"), you are owning your own experience, and the other person is often able to hear you more easily.

3. Recognize the needs that you wish to meet.

Needs are at the core of NVC. Your needs are what you care about, what matters most to you. Needs can range from the fundamental need for food or shelter to the need for freedom, dignity, self-expression, meaning, or connection. Coming to understand your own needs and to sense the needs that others are trying to meet is a pathway to transforming your experience and living more fully. When you understand and identify your needs—and you recognize that the other person is seeking to meet their needs *and* you try to understand what is driving them—you move toward resolving conflict rather than exacerbating it.

I experienced this when working with a company whose staff I had a very good relationship with but whose cancellation policy, I felt, was overly legalistic. When I sat with my feelings of annoyance and a belief that "This isn't fair," I saw that underlying them was a wish for clarity and understanding. I really wanted to understand more clearly the rationale for the decision they were making.

Mindfulness helps you connect with your own needs—what matters most to you—and bring curiosity and empathy to inquire into what the other person needs in this situation.

4. Make requests.

Ask for what you are seeking rather than making demands or implicit suggestions (for example, "Could you give me a call to tell me if you'll be getting home late this evening?" Compare this to, "I hope you're not going to spend all evening with your friends again"). When you make clear requests, you communicate to the other person what you need. They are free to say yes or no—and if they say no, you can invite further discussion of your needs and theirs and/or explore other ways you might get your needs met.

Can you envision how bringing a mindfulness-based approach to NVC might help you change harmful habits of communication and cultivate more beneficial ones?

Bring NVC to Life

Think of a recent situation when you were involved in a tense or difficult conversation—with a family member, friend, work colleague, or other. Reflect on the situation: where you were; when; what was done and said; how you felt before, during, and after; what you've thought about the situation since. Hold all that has arisen in kind awareness.

Think about engaging again with this person: How would you speak about what happened—and what triggered or annoyed you—in a nonjudgmental way and in the language of *observations*? (For example, "When I shared personal information with you and asked you to keep it confidential, you then shared it with X...")

State kindly and without judgment your *feelings*. (For example, "I felt angry... sad... annoyed... when you shared information that we agreed was confidential with X...")

Explore within yourself what your deepest *need* is in this situation. In the case of a friend sharing private information, the need might be for trust, consideration, safety, or respect. How might you share this need with the other person? (For example, "I want to feel trust between us and when...")

Envision a way of expressing a *request* that would meet your need. (For example, "When I share confidential information with you, can you agree to keep it to yourself?")

As you reflect on how you might speak of what you felt or feel, what you need, and what you are asking of the other person, invite an empathic curiosity in yourself to what the other person might be needing in this situation. See if you can put yourself in their experience—what they might have been sensing, feeling, needing... What questions might you ask to deepen your own understanding of what the other person was experiencing and might need? Can you enter the conversation as fully present as you can with your own experience and be open, caring, and compassionate toward the other person and their needs?

Using the Buddha's teachings on wise speech and Marshall Rosenberg's approach of nonviolent communication, we can transform long-standing habits of communication, deepen inner ease and well-being, and cultivate mutual support and harmony in our relations with others.

CHAPTER 11

Bringing Our Habits Above the Line

It is the nature of habits to start as largely conscious and purpose-driven actions—and to become unconscious, automatic, and triggered by situation and context. So in order to change habits that are not benefiting us, we need first to bring them into conscious awareness—above the line dividing what is conscious from what is unconscious.

With some habits, this may be relatively straightforward to do; for example, we may be completely aware of how often we smoke as well as the price we pay for it. But in other cases, our habits may be trickier and elusive.

In this chapter, we'll explore how mindfulness can help us work with habits that are challenging to many: procrastination, negative thinking and beliefs, and unconscious thoughts and actions that are part of our unexamined assumptions about the world.

The Habit of Procrastination

Procrastination is a familiar habit to many of us. We know it's important to get something done (work on our taxes, finish a report, or organize our office, for example) but we keep putting it off. Chronic procrastination affects 25 percent of the adult population (Burka and Yuen 2008) and has destructive effects on mental and physical health. It can lead to chronic stress, symptoms of depression and anxiety, feelings of shame and guilt, and negative health behaviors (Lieberman 2019; Wohl, Pychyl, and Bennett 2010).

Procrastination is a self-defeating behavior. We know we are paying a price for not acting on what is important but still do it—or don't. It's a way of avoiding unpleasant emotions and moods. When we procrastinate we are choosing short-term benefits—avoiding unpleasant feelings such as tedium, anxiety, or self-doubt—over the longer-term benefits of achieving our goals. We get a reward of momentary relief from putting off an unpleasant task or responsibility, and the reward encourages us to repeat the behavior, leading it easily to become a chronic habit. Our choice of short-term rewards over long-term costs (which normally far outweigh the rewards) arises from our evolutionary tendency to prioritize short-term needs ahead of long-term ones.

"We really weren't designed to think ahead into the further future because we needed to focus on providing for ourselves in the here and now," according to Dr. Hal Hershfield, of UCLA's Anderson School of Management (Lieberman 2019). Procrastination can be seen as an example of the ancient part of our brain overriding our more modern prefrontal cortex, discussed in chapter 2. The threat-detector part of our brain, the amygdala, perceives the task we are putting off as a genuine threat—and our brain is more concerned about removing the threat than about the potential long-term costs (of not carrying out the task).

Mindfulness—along with self-forgiveness and self-compassion practices—can provide a powerful antidote for dealing with procrastination by bringing into awareness the unpleasant feelings that we try to escape through procrastination. Mindfulness, self-forgiveness, and self-compassion impart healthier alternatives to putting off the task.

Working Skillfully with Procrastination

After all that we've learned about mindfulness, we might simply conclude that being focused on the present—on the unpleasant feelings associated with the task we're working hard to avoid—rather than on the future benefits of getting the task done is a more mindful approach. But rather than opening to the unpleasant feelings with kindness and acceptance, and letting them come and go, we are actually resisting the unpleasant feelings by putting off the task at hand. And studies have shown that procrastination is negatively associated with mindfulness—as procrastination increases, mindfulness decreases, and vice versa (Sirois and Tosti 2012).

As researchers Sirois and Tosti note, "The low mindfulness associated with procrastination indicates that the quality of the present-oriented focus... is not one that is truly present or accepting of current experiences" (2012, 12). They continue, pointing to the way that mindfulness can provide a skill to work with habits of procrastination:

> Difficult tasks can activate judgmental and reactive thoughts which promote judgment, self-criticism, and impulsive decisions to abandon the task. In contrast, mindfulness facilitates non-reactive acknowledgment and acceptance of these difficult thoughts and allows them to dissipate. (2012, 12)

In bringing mindfulness to the habit of procrastinating, it is critical to meet the unpleasant feelings that habitually lead us to put off doing what we know is important to do with kindness and acceptance. Let's take a typical example:

Monica is habitually late in filing her taxes. In recent years she's paid significant penalties and interest on what she owes for late filing. But despite the costs of avoiding the task, she finds ways of putting it off. The thought that she *should* work on her taxes comes to mind frequently, but other thoughts of how much work will be involved, how long it will take, and how tedious the work will be lead her to inaction. She feels immediate relief in not having to get started. Yet Monica is also regularly aware of the gnawing thoughts in her mind and the tightness in her chest and stomach when she thinks about her taxes.

Using mindfulness to work with her habit of procrastinating, an alternative and more helpful way of responding opens up:

Monica begins by pausing and bringing awareness to the unpleasant thoughts and feelings associated with working on her taxes: feelings of anxiety and boredom, tension in her chest and belly, negative thoughts about how she doesn't like working on her taxes, and fear of not being able to find all the documents and receipts she needs. Slowing down and not acting on her thoughts and feelings, Monica makes space for the feelings, letting them come and go in their own time without resistance or judgment. She observes her thoughts without latching on to them. Monica chooses to let them come and go.

She asks herself, *Is it really true that I'll never be able to find all the documents I need? Or that it will take forever to get the taxes finished?* Monica chooses to replace self-doubt and self-judgment with kindness and nonjudgment, providing herself with a *reward* of pleasant feelings (kindness, acceptance, nonjudgment) to replace the unpleasant feelings that unconsciously lead her to put off working on her taxes.

Bringing Self-Forgiveness and
Self-Compassion to Procrastination

Another approach Monica can use is to forgive herself for not working on her taxes. A 2010 study by Michael Wohl and colleagues found that students who were able to forgive themselves for procrastinating when studying for one exam procrastinated less when studying for their next exam. The researchers concluded, "Forgiveness allows the individual to move past their maladaptive behavior and focus on the upcoming examination without the burden of past acts to hinder studying" (Wohl, Pychyl, and Bennett 2010, 806).

By realizing that their behavior was "a transgression against the self" and letting go of negative feelings, they were able to start fresh in preparing for the next exam, without carrying baggage from the past. The students were able to replace an *avoidance* behavior (focused on avoiding stress, worry, doubt, and the like) with an *approach* behavior (focused on exam preparation) (Wohl, Pychyl, and Bennett 2010).

The related practice of self-compassion has also been shown to decrease procrastination. In a 2012 study of four samples of students, the trait of procrastination was associated with lower levels of self-compassion and higher levels of stress. The research suggested that "lower levels of self-compassion may explain some of the stress experienced by procrastinators, and interventions that promote self-compassion could therefore be beneficial for these individuals" (Sirois 2012, 128).

A practice to support Monica in dealing with her procrastination would include bringing mindfulness to her direct experience, as discussed above, then to forgive herself for her behavior. She might say to herself kindly, *I recognize that not working on my taxes was unwise and has caused me mental suffering as well as other painful consequences. I extend a full and heartfelt forgiveness to myself. I forgive myself.* She might then fully commit herself to working on her taxes (in ways discussed below).

Alternatively, or in combination with self-forgiveness, Monica could use the practice of self-compassion to work with her habit of procrastination. She could begin by bringing kind and nonjudgmental awareness to her feelings, sensations, thoughts, and emotions, and then send wishes of compassion to herself. She might say, *May I be happy… May I be safe… May I be kind to myself… May I accept myself as I am.* And then make a commitment to working diligently on her taxes in ways we will now discuss.

More Ways to Stop the Procrastination Habit

With these foundations of mindfulness, self-forgiveness, and self-compassion, other helpful practices can help ensure that we actualize our intentions.

One simple approach is to commit to working a specific amount of time each day on the task—the more specific the intention, the more likely we are to be successful. So the commitment might be, *When I get home from work and have eaten supper, I will work for thirty minutes on my taxes before relaxing and watching TV.*

Another approach is to break down the task into smaller chunks and work for a given amount of time on the chunk that is next in line. Referring back to chapter 8 and asking yourself, *What will make this task easier, more obvious, more attractive, or more satisfying?* can also help make something that is perceived as unpleasant or problematic more approachable. It can be as simple as promising yourself you will do something pleasant or fun once you have finished working on your taxes.

Working Mindfully with Negative Thoughts

How do you typically respond when you experience adversity, from losing your job to your computer freezing? Do you tend to believe, *I'm never going to be able to get a job... This is always happening to me... Nothing ever goes right for me... I might as well not try...?* Or do you respond by thinking, *Stuff happens... I'll be able to get it fixed... Find another job... Things will work out...?*

The habitual ways that we explain to ourselves why events happen—our "explanatory style" (Abramson, Seligman, and Teasdale 1978)—has a significant impact on our happiness and well-being. Those with a *pessimistic explanatory style* tend to interpret positive events in their lives as a product of causes that are external (*It wasn't my fault*), unstable (*It won't last*), and specific (*It won't have an impact on other areas of my life*). Conversely, negative events are interpreted as internal (*It was all my fault*), stable (*It will last forever*), and global (*This is going to impact other areas of my life*).

For a person with an *optimistic explanatory style*, these attributions will be reversed—positive events being viewed as due to one's efforts or talents, as likely to last, and as likely to have a positive impact in other areas.

These ways of explaining our experiences are not immutable. They are learned habits of thinking, often developed from a young age to understand and explain to ourselves adverse experiences. They can be changed through training and practice. Martin Seligman, a leader in the field of positive psychology, argues that just as we can learn from experience to give up hope and not act to change our circumstances (learned helplessness), we can learn optimism: "[T]eaching optimism to your children is as important as teaching them to work hard or be truthful, for it can have just as profound an impact on their later lives" (Seligman 2006, 234).

The way we respond to our habits of thinking significantly affects whether we develop other positive and beneficial habits or unhealthy ones. Our response has a profound impact on our well-being and happiness. If we take our thoughts as a given, as though they are the truth, then habits of thinking we developed in childhood can become the template with which we interpret later experiences of adversity. This was my experience when, as a two-year-old, I was quarantined in the hospital for scarlet fever for three weeks. The belief of my two-year-old mind that I'd been abandoned by my parents affected my feelings of safety and trust for a long time afterward.

Pessimistic habits of thinking can lead to depression and to failing to take care of ourselves (for example, avoiding cultivating healthy habits because *What difference would it make?*). If we view these habits of thinking as changeable, we can abandon negative and pessimistic habits of thinking and replace them with more affirmative and optimistic thinking, using mindfulness and cognitive approaches that dispute negative habits of thinking.

Bringing Mindfulness to Our Automatic Negative Thoughts

We can take time in meditation and in our daily lives to observe our patterns of thinking. Find a relaxed and comfortable posture. Take a few longer, deeper breaths to help yourself settle. And bring awareness to the thoughts that come up. Ask yourself:

- Are my thoughts harsh, critical, or judgmental toward myself?

- Do I blame myself for what happens—in an automatic rather than discerning way?

- Do I generalize from a particular experience, such as thinking, "This is always happening"?

- Do I think this is never going to change?

With mindfulness, you can observe thoughts as thoughts rather than as the truth. Say to yourself, *That's a negative thought*, and then let it pass. Check in with your bodily feelings and emotions. Allow yourself to feel what's present (for example, sadness, tension, or overwhelm) with kindness. Make space for these feelings, letting them come and go in their own time.

You might also invite in a wish of kindness and compassion toward yourself. Say, *May I be happy… May I be kind to myself… May I accept myself just as I am…*

Mindfulness brings our thoughts into awareness, allowing us to see them as impermanent phenomena that we can, with practice, loosen our identification with.

Using Cognitive Approaches to Disrupt Negative Thinking

Mindfulness practices for working with thoughts can be supported by approaches of *cognitive therapy*, a type of psychotherapy in which negative patterns of thinking about ourselves and the world are challenged. It is used to address a wide range of mental health conditions. Cognitive therapy focuses on addressing the psychological distress experienced, while cognitive behavioral therapy (CBT) focuses on eliminating the negative behaviors. Cognitive therapy uses five tactics:

1. **Recognize the automatic thought.** See your automatic negative thoughts as *learned explanations* that may be *permanent, pervasive,* and/or *personal.* Learned explanations are understandings we have drawn from our experience. For example, if you learned as a child that minor setbacks (such as not getting selected for a sports team or witnessing a parent not getting a job promotion) are akin to catastrophic failure, you might receive a college rejection letter and you say to yourself, *I'm never going to get accepted anywhere. I'm just not smart enough to go to college.* Recognize this thinking as a negative thought, that the thought of "never" being able to get into college makes this one situation permanent

and pervasive, and that the single decision by one college has led to negative personal thoughts about not being smart enough.

2. **Dispute the automatic thought.** Focus on evidence that contradicts your automatic thinking. For example, reflect on how well you did in many of your classes and the fact that this was the most difficult college to get into.

3. **Provide different explanations.** Consider how you can reattribute the factors in the incident. For example, you might consider, *My grades may not have been good enough for the college that didn't accept me, but I have a good chance in the other schools. If things don't work out this time round I can go back to the drawing board.*

4. **Learn to distract yourself.** Rather than ruminating on the negative thought, you might choose to put your attention into some other activity for a time. Take a walk, engage in something physical like yoga or stretching, listen to music, and more. You can go back to thinking about the incident when you feel ready.

5. **Recognize and question the assumptions that underpin your thinking.** Your automatic negative

thoughts often have an underlying fear or other uncomfortable emotion or belief attached to them. Without awareness, this underlying experience is hard to identify. But if you can pause and explore what underpins your thinking, you can better address the root of the problem rather than its symptoms. Going back to step 1, if your automatic negative thought was *I'm never going to get accepted anywhere; I'm just not smart enough to go to college,* you can practice questioning what is underlying the thought—perhaps a learned belief that you're not good enough and will fail at whatever you do.

Keep bringing these thoughts and beliefs into awareness, recognizing and disputing them, and putting forward other explanations that dispute the automatic thoughts and beliefs. As you keep recognizing and disputing the learned, habitual thought, you come to see more clearly that they are simply learned explanations and that they do not serve you.

Mindfulness can support us in questioning our automatic negative thoughts by providing the skills to help us stay with the difficult emotions and feelings that arise in connection with the negative thought process. When we bring awareness to our habits of thinking, we can break the cycle that keeps us in negative habit loops. We can then evaluate our experience with discernment—rather than interpreting it through the prism of past events.

Bringing Mindfulness to Unconscious Beliefs and Assumptions

In our discussions so far we've largely focused on habits that we are fairly aware of and want to change. For instance, the thought *I don't like the fact that I spend so much time on social media when I have more important things to do* is readily in our consciousness. We may, however, have other habits that we are not aware of that cause harm to ourselves or others and impact our well-being.

Some of these unexamined habits form part of what has been called our *assumptive world*—the way we have been acculturated and conditioned to view the world. For O'Connor (2014, 13), "The assumptive world includes our most basic beliefs—conscious and unconscious—about how the world works, and the particular lenses we see the world through. It's the givens we were born with—our race, our class, our gender, our nationality—and how they bias our point of view. It's much of what we absorbed unconsciously from our parents and our childhood interactions..."

If you are a man, you might have developed habits of speaking (for example, being one of the first to speak in a group, speaking longer than most other speakers, being prone to interrupt others, and so on) that you consider are just part of your communication style. You may not be aware of the harm your habits cause or the way they may have come out of and reinforce gender inequities.

189

If you are a white person, you might believe that racism and inequities based on race are no longer a significant issue, that we now have a level playing field, and that you can be fair and color blind in your treatment of people of all races. Yet these are also assumptive beliefs that have been part of your family and social conditioning; they fail to address the continued reality and pain of race and racism in our society.

On a more individual level, you may have internalized certain views about yourself. For instance, you may believe that you are unlovable, a failure, or a golden child by how you were treated in your family—and you may carry these views about yourself with you in your relationships in adult life.

Recalling Jung's statement that "What is not brought into consciousness comes to us as fate," how do we bring our unexamined assumptions about ourselves and the world into awareness so that we can choose to change what needs to be changed?

Bringing the Unconscious into Awareness

Try this practice to become clearer about your "assumptive world." Begin by getting quiet and turning your attention inward and asking:

- Where am I causing harm to myself or others through my thoughts, words, or actions?

- Where are my thoughts, words, or actions out of alignment with my deepest intentions and values?

- What might I be missing?

As you sit with these questions, pay close attention to what you are feeling in your body. There might be a feeling of tightness in the belly or ripples of fear or anxiety moving through your torso. Notice if there is anything unclear or fuzzy about the sensation, if something seems to be calling for attention.

Eugene Gendlin (1981), who developed the approach of Focusing, calls this unclear or fuzzy feeling the "felt sense." In the Focusing approach, we sense into the body, see what is calling for attention, and with a kind and curious awareness stay with what is present and say hello to what is here. Next, we describe the felt sense (for example, tightness, squeezing, or heaviness) and inquire of the body and the felt sense whether this is an accurate description.

Go back and forth between the word or phrase and the felt sense. Sit with kind curiosity and sense how the felt sense (tightness, squeezing, et cetera) feels, from your body's point of view. Let the felt sense change, if it does. And see if the word or phrase describing the felt sense changes.

Out of this empathic engagement with your own experience may come releases of holding, understanding of the cause of inner tension, or greater openness and a sense of freedom.

Engaging in this way with our bodily experience helps us open to habits that are causing us harm—habits that our minds can't untangle but that our bodies just *know*. This can help bring us to awareness of what is causing harm and how to find our way to greater health and well-being.

We can also become aware of unconscious and unexamined habits by paying close attention to the feedback we are getting from others. This may not always be direct—someone might be angry with you for one of your habitual behaviors without even being aware of what is triggering them. But their anger or annoyance can be information that something is calling for attention. You might ask yourself kindly and nonjudgmentally, *What is it in me that seems to have triggered this response?*

Finally, we can choose to broaden our awareness of our assumptive world, particularly in areas of race, class, gender identity, and sexual orientation. As well, we can look at areas where privilege comes to some with the luxury of not having to pay attention to it, while others, less privileged, wake up every day to inequity and harm. Compassionate and nonjudgmental curiosity is an important attitude and skill to bring to this engagement, so that you can hold with kindness any feelings of blame, shame, or other painful emotions that arise when you open yourself to what was formerly hidden from your view.

The habits explored in this chapter can bring up challenging emotions and mind states. Understanding the deep roots of these habits and holding ourselves and others with compassion and kindness can be a powerful support as we move our habits *above the line*. The gain we achieve for the effort we make comes to us as connection, love, and wholeness. To invert the earlier quote from Jung, what we bring to consciousness opens us to ever greater freedom.

Conclusion

The renowned Vietnamese Zen teacher, author, poet, and activist Thich Nhat Hanh spoke of the "miracle of mindfulness" and wrote a book by this title. The "miracle" is not supernatural or otherworldly. It is deeply human and available to us all. It is the freedom, joy, and peace that come from meeting this moment wholeheartedly, with kindness and acceptance. The miracle, says Thich Nhat Hanh (1996), is not to walk on water, but "to walk on the green earth, dwelling deeply in the present moment and feeling truly alive."

In bringing mindfulness to our habits, the "miracle" is that we bring what has become unconscious into conscious awareness. When we bring our habitual actions and thoughts into awareness, we make a space between stimulus and response. We can then consciously choose to act in ways that serve our well-being and happiness.

Some of the keys to transforming our habits through mindfulness that we've explored include:

- Understanding how habits form, why they can be hard to change, and the role mindfulness plays in habit change

- Cultivating and deepening the bedrock habit of meditation and daily life mindfulness

- Addressing habits at their roots and meeting these energies with acceptance rather than acting them out or suppressing them

- Changing the channel from painful or harmful mind states to those—like compassion and gratitude—that lead to well-being

- Bringing mindfulness to habits that don't serve us, such as unhealthy eating or drinking, mindlessness in use of devices and technology, harmful speech, and procrastination

- Developing beneficial habits that lead to greater happiness and peace, like mindful speech, healthy consuming, exercise, and adequate sleep

We can bring mindfulness to abandon any unhelpful habit that does not serve. And we can mindfully cultivate habits—such as meditation, exercising, eating consciously, and using technology and our devices wisely—to enhance our lives. Whatever the habit, the steps to work with it are consistent:

- Scan your behaviors, assess their harm or benefits, and **identify** a habit to cultivate or abandon.

- Connect with your **intention** to make change in this area. Ask yourself, *How serious is my commitment to working to develop or abandon this habit?* Cultivate and deepen your intention if this is a habit that is important for you to change.

- Pay close **attention** to how an existing habit gets acted out—when, where, with whom, and so forth—and envision the conditions that will support you in developing a new habit. Be curious about the habit and interested in it. Open to and work with the feelings associated with the habit. Meet lapses with kindness and diligence.

- Bring **awareness** to the strategies and approaches you will take to prevent the arising of an unhealthy habit. Think about ways you can work with the unhealthy habit *before*, *during*, and *after* it appears. Envision steps to make a new healthy habit *easier, more obvious, attractive, or satisfying*—and the opposite in the case of a habit you wish to abandon.

- **Commit** to carrying out the new behavior for a set period (a week, for example) and keep a day-by-day record of steps you have taken to develop or change this habit. If possible, make yourself accountable to someone; report to them how things have gone. At the end of the set period, make a commitment for another period, and continue until the new habit is formed or the old one abandoned.

Finally, as the Dalai Lama consistently urges: Never give up. It is our nature to lapse and forget at times, but with training and diligence, we can always come back and begin again. The more we come back and the more we keep repeating the helpful behavior, the more we create the conditions to live consciously, intentionally, and freely. It's never too late to start. We can always come back to this breath, this feeling, this moment.

Acknowledgments

I'm grateful for the support of many people in writing this book. My gratitude to all those whose teachings and practice have helped to keep these precious teachings alive and a true refuge for twenty-five centuries; to teachers, mentors, friends, and colleagues who have helped clarify my understanding or improve my writing, including Tara Brach, Jonathan Foust, Jack Kornfield, Sharon Salzberg, Ruth King, Rick Hanson, Pat Coffey, Kristin Barker, Kathleen Gless, Ola Witkowska, Stephanie Kohler, Helen Barley, Gene Kijowski, Sharon Bauer, Lisa Haskins, and Brian Levy; everyone at New Harbinger Publications, especially Wendy Millstine, Vicraj Gill, Jess O'Brien, and Marisa Solís; friends, students, and fellow teachers of the Insight Meditation Community of Washington (IMCW); friends who generously offered their beautiful homes to stay in and write, including Sara Shelley and Rich Weinfeld, Patti Elledge and George, Peter Sawchyn and Chin Mah, and many friends in Indian Rocks Beach, Florida; and all who have provided love and emotional support, including my daughter, Emma, her husband, John, and my grandchildren, John, Hugh, and Eve; my son, Joe; my siblings, their partners, and families in London and other parts of the UK, Barcelona, Australia, and the United States; my mother, who died during the writing and whose life is a source of gratitude; my late father; and my life partner, Rebecca Hines, who has supported me in a million ways, including gracefully putting up with me working on the last book I write on a deadline.

References

Abramson, L., M. Seligman, and J. Teasdale. 1978. "Learned Helplessness in Humans: Critique and Reformulation." *Journal of Abnormal Psychology* 87(1): 49–74.

Alter, A. 2017. *Irresistible: The Rise of Addictive Technology and the Business of Keeping Us Hooked.* New York: Penguin Books.

Associated Press. 2015a. "30 Percent of Americans Have Had an Alcohol-Use Disorder." *Newsweek* June 3. https://www.newsweek.com/30-percent-americans-have-had-alcohol-use-disorder-339085.

Associated Press. 2015b. "33 Million Americans Are Problem Drinkers, or 14 Percent of U.S. Adults." *Washington Post* June 8. https://www.washingtonpost.com/national/health-science/33-million-americans-are-problem-drinkers-or-14-percent-of-us-adults/2015/06/08/b75c4854-0af4-11e5-95fd-d580f1c5d44e_story.html?utm_term=.05cd56922f82.

Blumenthal, B. 2015. *52 Small Changes for the Mind.* San Francisco: Chronicle Books.

Bodhi, B. 1995. *The Middle Length Discourses of the Buddha: A New Translation of the Majjhima Nikaya.* Original translation by Bhikkhu Ñanamoli. Boston: Wisdom Publications.

Bodhi, B. 2000. *The Noble Eightfold Path: Way to the End of Suffering.* Onalaska, WA: Buddhist Publication Society.

Boone, J. L., and J. P. Anthony. 2003. "Evaluating the Impact of Stress on Systemic Disease: The MOST Protocol in Primary Care." *Journal of the American Osteopathic Association* 3(105): 239–246. http://163.178.103.176/Fisiologia/Integra/Objetivo7/Impactodelestres.pdf.

Brach, T. 2012. *True Refuge: Finding Peace and Freedom in Your Own Awakened Heart.* New York: Bantam.

Burka, J. and L. Yuen. 2008. *Procrastination: Why You Do It, What to Do About It Now.* Cambridge, MA: Perseus Books.

Byrne, H. 2016. *The Here-and-Now Habit: How Mindfulness Can Help You Break Unhealthy Habits Once and for All.* Oakland, CA: New Harbinger Publications.

CDC. 2018. "Smoking Is Down, but Almost 38 Million American Adults Still Smoke." Centers for Disease Control and Prevention. January 18. https://www.cdc.gov/media/releases/2018/p0118-smoking-rates-declining.html.

CDC. 2019. "Fast Facts: Diseases and Death." Centers for Disease Control and Prevention. February 6. https://www.cdc.gov/tobacco/data_statistics/fact_sheets/fast_facts/index.htm.

Clear, J. 2018. *Atomic Habits: An Easy and Proven Way to Build Good Habits and Break Bad Ones.* London: Random House.

Colier, N. 2016. *The Power of Off: The Mindful Way to Stay Sane in a Virtual World.* Boulder, CO: Sounds True.

Csikszentmihalyi, M. 1990. *Flow: The Psychology of Optimal Experience.* New York: Harper Collins.

Duhigg, C. 2012. *The Power of Habit: Why We Do What We Do in Life and Business.* New York: Random House.

Emmons, R. 2013. *Gratitude Works!* San Francisco: Jossey-Bass.

Farb, N., Z. Segal, H. Mayberg, J. Bean, D. McKeon, Z. Fatima, and A. Anderson. 2007. "Attending to the Present: Mindfulness Meditation Reveals Distinct Neural Modes of Self-Reference." *Social Cognitive and Affective Neuroscience* 2 (4): 313–22.

Frankl, V. 2006. *Man's Search for Meaning.* Part One translated by I. Lasch. Boston: Beacon Press.

Fredrickson, B. 2000. "Cultivating Positive Emotions to Optimize Health and Well-Being." *Prevention and Treatment* 3 (1).

Gendlin, E. 1981. *Focusing.* New York: Bantam Books.

Gollwitzer, P., and B. Schaal. 1998. "Metacognition in Action: The Importance of Implementation Intentions. *Personality and Social Psychology Review* 2 (2): 124–36.

Hanson, R. 2009. *Buddha's Brain: The Practical Neuroscience of Happiness, Love, and Wisdom.* With R. Mendius. Oakland, CA: New Harbinger Publications.

Hölzel, B., J. Carmody, M. Vangel, C. Congleton, S. Yerramsetti, T. Gard, and S. Lazar. 2011. "Mindfulness Practice Leads to Increases in Regional Brain Gray Matter Density." *Psychiatry Research: Neuroimaging* 191 (1): 36–43.

HSUS. N.d. "An HSUS Report: The Welfare of Animals in the Meat, Egg, and Dairy Industries." Humane Society of the United States. Accessed January 13, 2019. https://www.humane society.org/sites/default/files/docs/hsus-report-welfare-animals -meat-egg-dairy-industry.pdf.

Jackson, T., R. Dawson, and T. Wilson. 2003. "Case Study: Evaluating the Effect of Email Interruptions Within the Workplace." *International Journal of Information Management* 23 (1): 55–65.

James, W. 1890. *The Principles of Psychology*. New York: Henry Holt (reprinted Bristol: Thoemmes Press, 1999).

Kabat-Zinn, J. 2013. *Full-Catastrophe Living: Using the Wisdom of Your Body and Mind to Face Stress, Pain, and Illness*. New York: Bantam.

Kahneman, D. 2011. *Thinking, Fast and Slow*. New York: Farrar, Straus and Giroux.

Killingsworth and Gilbert. 2010. "A Wandering Mind Is an Unhappy Mind." *Science* 330: 932. http://www.danielgilbert .com/KILLINGSWORTH%20&%20GILBERT%20(2010).pdf.

Levine, P. 1997. *Waking the Tiger: Healing Trauma*. Berkeley, CA: North Atlantic Books.

Levitin, D. 2016. *The Organized Mind: Thinking Straight in the Age of Information Overload*. New York: Dutton.

Lieberman, C. 2019. "Why You Procrastinate (It Has Nothing to Do with Self-Control." *New York Times* March 25. https://www .nytimes.com/2019/03/25/smarter-living/why-you-procrastinate -it-has-nothing-to-do-with-self-control.html.

Lyubomirsky, S. 2007. *The How of Happiness: A New Approach to Getting the Life You Want*. New York: Penguin Books.

Maguire, E. A., K. Woollett, and H. Spiers. 2006. "London Taxi Drivers and Bus Drivers: A Structural MRI and Neuro-psychological Analysis." *Hippocampus* 16: 1,091–1,101.

Mingyur, Y. 2007. *The Joy of Living: Unlocking the Secret and Science of Happiness*. With E. Swanson. New York: Harmony Books.

Mirasol Recovery Centers. 2018. "Eating Disorder Statistics." Accessed February 19, 2019. https://www.mirasol.net/learning-center/eating-disorder-statistics.php.

Mischel, W. 2014. *The Marshmallow Test: Mastering Self-Control.* New York: Little, Brown and Company.

Mohd, R. S. 2008. "Life Event, Stress, and Illness." *The Malaysian Journal of Medical Sciences,* 15(4): 9–18. https://www.ncbi.nlm.nih.gov/pmc/articles/PMC3341916/.

NCSA (National Center for Statistics and Analysis). 2017. "Distracted Driving 2015." *Traffic Safety Facts Research Note. Report No. DOT HS 812 381.* Washington, DC: National Highway Traffic Safety Administration.

Nhat Hanh, T. 1995. *Be Still and Know: Reflections from "Living Buddha, Living Christ."* New York: Riverhead Books.

Nilsen, P., K. Roback, A. Bröstrom, and P. Ellström. 2012. "Creatures of Habit: Accounting for the Role of Habit in Implementation Research on Clinical Behavior Change." *Implementation Science* 7 (53): 1–6.

Nyanaponika Thera and Bhikkhu Bodhi. 1999. *Numerical Discourses of the Buddha: An Anthology of Suttas from the Anguttara Nikaya.* Walnut Creek, CA: Altamira Press.

O'Connor, R. 2014. *Rewire: Change Your Brain to Break Bad Habits, Overcome Addictions, Conquer Self-destructive Behavior.* New York: Penguin Books.

Pollan, M. 2009. *Food Rules: An Eater's Manual.* New York: Penguin Books.

Quinn, J., A. Pascoe, W. Wood, and D. Neal. 2010. "Can't Control Yourself? Monitor These Bad Habits." *Personality and Social Psychology Bulletin* 36 (4): 499–511.

Rogers, R. D., and S. Monsell. 1995. "Depth of Processing and the Retention of Words in Episodic Memory." *Journal of Experimental Psychology: General* 124 (2): 207–231.

Rosenberg, M. 2003. *Nonviolent Communication: A Language of Life*. Encinitas, CA: PuddleDancer Press.

Sapolsky, R. 2004. *Why Zebras Don't Get Ulcers*. New York: Owl Books.

Sirois, F. M., and N. Tosti. 2012. "Lost in the Moment? An Investigation of Procrastination, Mindfulness, and Well-Being. *Journal of Rational-Emotive and Cognitive-Behavior Therapy* 1–12.

Sofer, O. 2018. *Say What You Mean: A Mindfulness Approach to NVC*. Boulder, CO: Shambhala Publications.

Stahl C, B., and E. Goldstein 2010. *A Mindfulness-Based Stress Reduction Workbook*. Oakland, CA: New Harbinger Publications.

Tolle, E. 1999. *The Power of Now: A Guide to Spiritual Enlightenment*. Novato, CA: New World Library.

University of East Anglia. 2018. "It's Official: Spending Time Outside Is Good for You." *Science Daily*. July 6. https://www.sciencedaily.com/releases/2018/07/180706102842.htm.

Watson, J. M., and D. L. Strayer. 2010. "Supertaskers: Profiles in Extraordinary Multitasking Ability." *Psychonomic Bulletin and Review* 17 (4): 479–485.

WebMD. 2017. "The Effects of Stress on Your Body." Accessed February 22, 2019. https://www.webmd.com/balance/stress-management/effects-of-stress-on-your-body.

Wohl, M., T. A. Pychyl, and S. Bennett. 2010. "I Forgive Myself, Now I Can Study: How Self-Forgiveness for Procrastinating Can Reduce Future Procrastination." *Personality and Individual Differences* 48, 803–808.

Wood, W., and D. Neal. 2016. "Healthy Through Habit: Interventions for Initiating and Maintaining Health Behavior Change." *Behavioral Science and Policy* 2(1): 71–83.

Worldwatch. N.d. "Meat Production Continues to Rise." Worldwatch Institute: Washington, DC. http://www.world watch.org/node/5443.

Hugh G. Byrne, PhD, is a senior teacher with the Insight Meditation Community of Washington (IMCW), and cofounder of the Mindfulness Training Institute of Washington. He has worked extensively in the fields of human rights and social justice, and is committed to advocating the benefits of mindfulness and other contemplative practices to help relieve the suffering of the world. Byrne teaches classes, retreats, and workshops in the United States and internationally. He resides in Silver Spring, MD.

Real change *is* possible

For more than forty-five years, New Harbinger has published proven-effective self-help books and pioneering workbooks to help readers of all ages and backgrounds improve mental health and well-being, and achieve lasting personal growth. In addition, our spirituality books offer profound guidance for deepening awareness and cultivating healing, self-discovery, and fulfillment.

Founded by psychologist Matthew McKay and Patrick Fanning, New Harbinger is proud to be an independent, employee-owned company. Our books reflect our core values of integrity, innovation, commitment, sustainability, compassion, and trust. Written by leaders in the field and recommended by therapists worldwide, New Harbinger books are practical, accessible, and provide real tools for real change.

 newharbingerpublications

Also by Hugh Byrne

Whatever your harmful habit is— you have the power to break it

ISBN: 978-1626252370 | US $16.95

The Here-and-Now Habit offers powerful practices based in mindfulness and neuroscience to help you rewire your brain and finally break the habits that are holding you back from a meaningful life.

Register your **new harbinger** titles for additional benefits!

When you register your **new harbinger** title—purchased in any format, from any source—you get access to benefits like the following:

- Downloadable accessories like printable worksheets and extra content

- Instructional videos and audio files

- Information about updates, corrections, and new editions

Not every title has accessories, but we're adding new material all the time.

Access free accessories in 3 easy steps:

1. Sign in at NewHarbinger.com (or **register** to create an account).

2. Click on **register a book**. Search for your title and click the **register** button when it appears.

3. Click on the **book cover or title** to go to its details page. Click on **accessories** to view and access files.

That's all there is to it!

If you need help, visit:

NewHarbinger.com/accessories

new harbinger
CELEBRATING
40 YEARS